SHIFT
...moving toward God's perspective

SHIFT

...moving toward God's perspective

WENDY DELCOURT

"*If you can imagine a benevolent, whirling weather system, that pulls you into its passionate embrace, that is Wendy! With irresistible and charismatic velocity, Wendy captivates those in her path with her skilled use of storytelling. Time spent soaking in her generous stream of guidance, encourages and empowers fellow sojourners to rekindle or create anew stories of their own.*" —**Heather Parlane**, artist, poet, and cofounder of The South Art Project, a community of meaningful connection, fueled by the power of the Expressive Arts, Kelowna, British Columbia, Canada

"*Wendy's teaching on strengths and leadership is a valued and memorable class with our students. Our young adults grow more equipped with insight and understanding of their spiritual gifts and unique strengths. These are often discovered through sharing personal experiences and shaping opportunities in their lives. I am confident the students will implement the teaching and learning of these principles when leading others throughout their educational experiences, impactful relationships, and life careers.*" —**Michelle Collins,** Pursuit School Coordinator, Kelowna, BC

"*Weird and wonder-filled Wendy! She has the ability to light up a room and instantaneously make everyone in it feel loved, like you've just been given a warm hug. Wendy is a powerful teacher, encourager, and cheerleader who unhesitatingly believes in God's best for all those she meets. What I admire about Wendy is that she walks the walk with a buoyant, Godly stride in all areas of her life. She is deeply loved!*" —**Vivian Bonin,** artisan friend and "Journey" sister, Kelowna, BC

"*I have the joy of regularly witnessing the light and warmth that Wendy brings to people's lives. She simply fills the room with her energy, resolute belief and love for people, life, and Jesus. Wendy's amazing story not only spurs us on; it confirms that Godly compassion and strength are most perfectly formed and forged in fire.*" —**Glen Madden,** lead pastor of Willow Park Church South, Kelowna, BC

SHIFT
Copyright © 2021 by Wendy Delcourt
Published by Deep River Books
Sisters, Oregon
www.deepriverbooks.com

ISBN – 13: 9781632695666
Library of Congress Control Number: 2021910895

Printed in the USA

Cover and interior design by Robin Black, Inspirio Design
Cover image by Wendy Delcourt, a personal painting entitled, "Humanity"

Table of Contents

Dedication

This book is dedicated to Delster (aka husband Grant) my tender and faithful soul soldier. This book lives because of our daily coffees together talking about this thing called life through praying, dreaming, creating, and problem solving.

To my two beautiful daughters, Hannah and Madison, you truly take my breath away with your design and the way your lives inspire my heart daily, teaching me so much about humility, compassion, and courage. Thank you for your life-giving presence and impact forever and always.

And to my many, many teachers, friends, and family who pray for me, encourage me, and believe in the best of me; you have given me inspiration to write because of your wisdom and love. God is using all the seeds you sow in such meaningful ways in my life.

Much of this book is a compilation of soul reflections in my personal journaling inspired by the many leaders in my life experiences and how I conceptualized their teachings in a way that made sense to me on my journey of becoming.

Don't limit the miracles. Encounter devastating love!
—Wendy Delcourt

I love you all to infinity and beyond!

Introduction

A few months ago, I was sitting at the bedside of David Marshall, my friend Maureen's husband, in his hospice room days before he went home to be with Jesus. After enjoying a cold milkshake and sharing stories among family and friends, I had a few quiet moments alone with David.

David was the first face my husband and I saw when we first attended Willow Park South church. Funny enough, his face was the first we saw for months afterward, and this guy never forgot one detail of our lives that we shared with him. Jokingly, we called him "stalker Dave." We couldn't believe the gift of hospitality this man had and the joy he found in the presence of people.

Now, Dave was preparing to meet his maker in a mysterious transition that awaits us all. I sat beside him and asked, "Dave, you are now about to enter eternity, so what is it that you can leave with me while I am still in this world. What do I need to learn from you?"

He looked at me with intensity in his big, bright eyes and said, "Wendy, pray about everything and invite Jesus into the details of your life because he cares about every detail—even the mundane." He paused for a moment and then continued. "When people ask you about your faith, don't just repeat spiritual doctrine, but share a story with them about how Jesus became real and personal to you."

As he gave me his final advice, his eyes filled with tears, and he shared the miracle story of his granddaughter who changed his heart forever. So, I want to take this opportunity to honor David and share within these pages the times in my life when Jesus became personal to me and how those experiences shifted me into a deeper and richer knowledge of the devastating love of my Father in heaven.

There are so many sayings I can recall that repeatedly captured me in conversation or annoyed me due to their lack of relevance at the time. I remember the social dilemmas in high school being informed by the words, "These are the moments that shape your character." Or my dad would often say that "Anything worth doing is hard work." The classic coaching line through my athletic journey always stated, "If there is no pain, there is no gain."

My motivational seminars and team cheers always emphasized to push hard, live courageously, and win for yourself. One wise woman said to me once to "choose not to be offended," because it all ends up funny down the road or something more significant comes along that requires a bit more grit, patience, and perseverance, leaving the one previous challenge looking rather minor.

Another phrase echoed to me was, "Get uncomfortable. Comfort can be a dangerous place." "Try getting fired!" My mom would say from time to time. "You will understand when you have your own kids someday." Dad would emphasize that a busy life requires one to "Touch it once," meaning don't move whatever "it" is you're doing to the shelf, to the desk, to your pile, and back again. "Touch it once!"

Another classic piece of advice we may all identify with is the infamous saying, "You don't know what you've got until it is gone." And let's not forget, "Don't judge a book by its cover." The list goes on.

I may have many words or unique ways of articulating my life experiences, but the truth of it all is that the act of living has brought life to the truth of these phrases in profound and impactful ways. God has used words that many others have spoken into my life to shape me into a better version of myself. I am going to share some of my stories in hopes that they will stimulate a conversation with yourself. Perhaps they might even annoy you. But I hope they will move you to think beyond the scope of your understanding into the realm of possibility. Your life is the greatest story you can share. What you say and who you are matters!

In this book, I invite you to consider your perspective as you process events in your story—how you grow along the way and how you respond to opportunities on your own pilgrimage of discovery.

CHAPTER ONE

Encouragement

"It is important to remember that we all have magic inside us."
—J.K. Rowling

It's November 1, and I am still in my jammies—a rare occasion—thinking about my dad. His birthday is today, and he would have been eighty-three. It's funny how these special dates and occasions mark the soul for eternity when people have an impact on your life.

I often reflect, as I grow and age, what I've learned from his life and what I continue to learn from him. He was a pillar, a person who held me up in this journey called life. It has been an adjustment because he no longer walks alongside me, sharing my burdens or being an encouraging voice on the other end of the line. I am still inspired and moved by his words that encompassed powerful concepts for living my life strong and well.

I published my first chapter book eight years ago, thinking that it would encompass all I had to say. It's funny how, as I grow in my faith and challenge my perceptions through experience and knowledge of God, there seems to be so much more to say and share about myself, God, and what He is up to in my life. When we live believing every experience is our teacher, the learning never ends, and the conversations of our lives continue.

People often ask me what I do for a living, and I sometimes hesitate to respond, as I've pursued over fifteen different jobs since I graduated from university in 1993.

In the beginning, I subsidized my education as a lifeguard and a swim coach, loving the environment of physical performance, challenging the human body to reach its potential in power, strength, and endurance. I loved tapping into the psychology of an athlete and teaching the mental discipline required to perform and to celebrate the hard training put in between race days. I loved building the concept of team, the very essence of community, drawing first on our identity as unique creations of God. I loved exploring how our personal talents and gifts can bring great reward both individually and collectively.

I then moved on to teaching children in the classroom, my favorite being elementary school. I love this age. Young children still have an innate sense of wonder and curiosity that makes the experience of learning exciting and fearless. I informed the curriculum by writing lesson plans and learning new strategies; education has limitless opportunity to stimulate potential.

As my husband Grant and I grew our family, I owned and operated a daycare so I would be able to be with our daughters while still contributing to our household income. Plus, I could practice my skills in the areas I enjoyed so much. As time went on, I narrowed my focus from developing people in the athletic and scholastic realms to spiritual formation and leadership development.

So now I refer to myself as a "potentialist," using a variety of platforms such as teaching, public speaking, leadership formation, writing, philanthropy, and the culture of storytelling to help others identify the unique qualities of their own stories and creativity. If you would have asked my daughter Madison when she was younger what her mom did for a living, her response would have been, "My mommy does pleasure jobs and gives the money back!" Wow, kids say the darndest things!

At the age of fifty, I continue to learn that personal change is a community project requiring me to live a self-examined life, to be honest with my struggles, and to be intentional in creating a climate of grace in my relationships so that all of us will reach our potential. The bible declares that a new heart is shaped in us from endurance, forbearance, longsuffering, patience, and perseverance. If we choose to see these conditions as opportunities to become holy in God's sight, we can lean on the divine power of the Spirit to live before God when the struggle is amped up in our life circumstances.

The book of Hebrews 12:1-3 continues to set the stage of my daily motivations. Paul shared these words at a time when Jewish Christians were under severe persecution and never wavered in their faith, a condition that is real to all of us. He encouraged them to "stand strong in their faith," no matter the challenge or opposition they faced.

Paul uses the metaphor of a race to encourage us to endure in our gifting and commitment to Christ. Everywhere I go, whether work, community gatherings, or an adventure, I visualize this massive arena or football stadium filled with fans cheering me on. Paul references these fans as "a great cloud of witnesses." These fans are not just any type of fan, but they are the champions or heroes of faith. They have run the race of life and won. They have passed the torch to us and are cheering and encouraging us on, just like the crowd in a large sporting event.

Paul warns us about the hindrances, the things that entangle us along the way that may be neither right nor wrong, but they need to be recognized and removed so we can stay focused on Jesus. This run illustrates that we are always moving forward in the race that is mapped out for us, persevering in a steadfast goal, patiently enduring in faith, stamina, commitment, and discipline. Jesus is the perfect example of this perseverance.

My hope is to be an instrument of equipping others for this divine relay race called life, reminding others that it requires self-awareness, teamwork, mental mapping, and challenge. This relay race will never be in your comfort zone nor is the end of the challenge always known. Every person has his or her own leg of the journey to complete, and their desire and action will greatly impact their success in life. The elements that seem frightening, or impossible, are where self ends and God begins the good work. For all those people who are watching us, we hope they will be mystified or curious enough about our journey to look a little closer at this big picture of God and how he works in our lives.

As a "potentialist," I invite the reader through these illustrations to consider his or her own journey in the long race. How is your life going so far? Is something hindering your endurance or weighing you down? What is challenging you? What is entangling your race?

God made His plan clear. His plan involves us. Hebrews 13:20-21 says, "May the God of peace, who through the blood of the eternal covenant brought back from the dead our Lord Jesus, that great Shepherd of the sheep, equip you with everything good for doing his will, and may he work in us what is pleasing to him, through Jesus Christ, to whom be the glory forever and ever. Amen."

God chooses to use our natural gifting and design to bring His story and truth to the world. So, I feel it is our calling and privilege to walk out his purpose by faith and see how God will use our gifting. One of his gifts to me is a word gift—an ability to encourage others. One of the greatest gifts my dad left behind was some words, written with his hand, prayed through by his heart, and created with the intention to teach, to share the human journey, to open doors to plumb the depths of God's love for us in conversation and faith. Dad and I shared that ability.

Because of the impact of my dad's gifts on me, I write these words with him in mind as I pass on my own learning experiences to my family. I imagine my daughters will be curious about how their mom experienced life's ups and downs. I hope they see how people are the curriculum God uses for growth opportunity. God used many moments of struggle, joy, and mystery to show me more of who He is and how powerful His love can be. Human suffering, in any form, is an invitation from our loving God to something more substantial.

I like to call this more substantial thing "devastating love," the love that takes us beyond the scope of logic, words, or imagination. May you find within these pages concepts that compel a more substantial connection to your personal relationship to God. May this reflective read better equip you to run your race well.

CHAPTER TWO

The Story We Give Power To

*"I am not what happened to me,
I am what I choose to become."*
—Carl Jung

If we keep practicing and building on the timeless gift of story-telling, paying attention to diverse perspectives, yet to a common hope of humanity, through our personal journeys, our thinking will truly be transformed and our scope of understanding broadened. Therefore, I write to you some of my stories, the soul coffees, and walks that I have with the community and with God that help me grab a hold of His heart in meaningful and relevant ways in my pilgrimage of faith. This writing is my way of making sense of the tension in my life, and it allows me to form concepts that I can use to explain my "why" to my actions and my deeply held spiritual beliefs.

It amazes me how many people can gather and witness or participate in the same event but have such a different perspective on its substance and experience, leaving room for varied interpretations. Whether these occasions or events build, or defeat comes down to the story we choose to make of it, the filter through which we pay attention. There are endless resources that reference the process of "good thinking," but the bible teaches us that good thinking is possible with a Christ-like filter over what we pay attention to and the power of the Holy Spirit, the infinite source of wisdom and truth.

Philippians 4:8 encourages us in this way: "Finally, brothers, whatever is true, whatever is honorable, whatever is just, whatever is pure, whatever is lovely, whatever is commendable, if there is any excellence, if there is anything worthy of praise, think about these things."

The stories we choose to tell and those we choose to hear hold great power in our lives. The assumptions we draw from experience and how we walk them out has consequences on our measure of a fulfilled life.

When I was a young girl, my dad seemed to be that guy who never failed, the one who could carry the weight of the world and still be okay. He was always there, his words were powerful, and his presence was noticed. Every day he dressed in his crisply ironed shirt and tie to head into the world of BC Gas, managing a demographic area and all its people and transitions within it.

He was mentally sharp and hung out with smart people. He was invited into many leadership roles in our community from serving in the Knights of Columbus, to coaching the local junior hockey team, to youth leader, and more.

Still, he provided for our family in ways where we never felt lack. He managed to keep our yard immaculate and designed it as a children's playground with safe spaces to run, paths to wander, trees to climb, fishponds to explore, a garden full of fresh veggies, and flowers that smiled at the sunshine as they thrived in such a space. He always came home and had dinner with the family, managed a run or walk, and still knelt by my bedside every night to pray. Yes, the memory that lives forever in my heart is that of my dad praying beside me as I pretended to be asleep.

Fast forward sixteen years to a phone call I received at university in 1988, close to Easter time, sharing with me that my dad had just had a massive heart attack. What? I completed my exams and came home to a much different picture of my dad; he was smaller, sunken, tired, slower, and his face told a different kind of story. Tears rolled down his eyes when he saw me. As he hugged me, he invited me back home, now a small apartment for he and my mom with little responsibility for upkeep, a warm bed, and lots of food in the fridge. His step was slower, and he didn't talk much. Who was this man?

As the years marched on, I watched my dad spend his time in the wilderness, wandering, looking for purpose, struggling and wrestling with his new disability. Now he carried a damaged heart. He was more emotional about everything and wavered about the ideal of a faithful God.

My dad could no longer perform for the self-worth he seemed to desperately seek. He no longer had the capacity to rush in as everyone's hero, so he was no longer invited to the corporate circles as a visionary and leader. He now tended a home and spent time with his grandchildren. Sometime during the day, he made a trip to some local coffee shop around Castlegar where he enjoyed reading the paper while he drank his coffee.

At times, I imagine he felt as though he was being punished for all he did wrong in his life—a bit of a shame walk. How he made sense of his life at this point portrayed a God that I didn't really like. A God that kept score, one who expected him to do all things, one who tormented his soul if he lived outside of the Lord's moral code. Where was this God of grace? Why wouldn't my dad go to church anymore? Why had he pulled away from friends and gathering places and allowed his world to shrink?

Not too long after Dad's major transition, dealing with the aftereffects of a damaged heart, I entered a dark time as well. I commenced on a journey of many years during which I endured exploratory surgeries, only to finally discover that I suffered from a rare disorder and how I would deal with it the rest of my life.

In this serial time and place, the man who knelt beside my bed and prayed for me as a child—my faithful prayer warrior—returned. My hospital room was filled with laughter, peppermint foot cream, and treats on my bedside table to bribe the nurses at night to make me feel more comfortable. It wasn't long until everyone knew my dad, and my dad radiated joy.

As I look back, I realize we can never know whose eyes God uses to watch over you, and how much we all crave in the depths of our hearts to be deeply noticed. At my bedside, Dad was deeply noticed by others who suffered and our caregivers. I realized his outpouring of kindness gave him such fulfillment. To this day, I ponder the true source of fulfillment and well-being.

My dad grew up in Humboldt, Saskatchewan, Canada on a small farm with eight kids during the Great Depression. He had five sisters and two brothers. When I was young, he taught me how to curl my hair. The habits of those five sisters came in handy. During his childhood, life was challenging. He did his chores, worked hard on the farm, went to school when he was able, and after a big meal, he went to bed. It was a time of survival and hard work.

My dad left home at about the age of fifteen to pursue his hockey dream. His decision took him to many new places and new faces to fill in for hockey players who were injured or off the ice for some reason. But it never really earned him a permanent place on any team.

I often think of his journey—a young man staying in boarding rooms, traveling around Canada and the US, never really putting down roots, trying to make a way for himself. He was quite a loner and had few people who mentored him or spoke wisdom into his life. He was always the one who had to work super hard for everything since he didn't have any family support or resources.

How did his hardships inform his life? From my perspective and after years of watching him, it seems as though it created a man who based his self-worth on performance rather than God's grace. He over performed in every endeavor to maintain his position of respect and to secure his future. But where was everyone he worked hard for when his body failed him? When he could no longer provide all those services? This changed me—awakened me to the brokenness of my dad and others, creating a time of transition and adjustment for me. I questioned the intentions of people who walked alongside my dad when he was strong. Now I found I could no longer turn to my dad for answers here.

As my dad journeyed through these transitional years, he sunk into a deep depression, even to the point of attempting to take his own life. On two of these occasions, I was by his side. The very thing I feared or could never imagine as a young girl who saw her dad as a hero, was a possibility. I realized he was human; he felt life deeply.

Not only did my dad crash mentally and physically from the imbalance of serotonin in his brain, partly caused by all of the concussions he suffered playing hockey, but also from losing touch with grace and believing the lie that his identity existed only through achievement. He desperately wanted to know hope and recover his spiritual connection. It was at this time when God provided and equipped me with Scripture and words I didn't even know I had. My Father in heaven intervened in my life when I came to the end of myself. He was fully present when I feared losing the man that I held so deeply in my heart and loved more than most. God met my dad and I together, drawing us into His presence in ways that my words cannot truly capture.

I remember looking into my dad's tear-filled eyes and repeating Scripture verses about how much God loved him, delighted in him, created him for a deeper purpose. I told him that every one of his tears mattered to God. His pain mattered to God. God noticed him when others didn't. God heard my dad's every cry from deep in his soul. God's Spirit prayed on his behalf, stood in the gap between him and the Father, inviting my dad into a divine purpose that only Jesus can offer. God gave him the hope that is only found in Christ—a love so devastating it transformed his soul and invited him into the place called grace.

Over some lonely times and long nights, my family eventually noticed that my dad demonstrated peace growing within him. Slowly, we could see a softening of his heart, and a gentle giver and person of selflessness emerged. Dad didn't lord his position or opinion over others. He gave compassionately; he showed up and met others where they were at; he prayed faithfully; he drew away from the crowd to spend many days with his Savior; and he came to church with us again. Dad joined the community in laughter and adventure and good soul coffee. He found joy in the mundane, and he lived to love children—the least of these. He loved! The lies Dad believed were being covered by a redeeming presence.

Don't get me wrong, a saint though he was, he could still sound off at the referee during a hockey game when my brother, Grant, had his team on the ice.

Dad was a man on a mission for justice and always struggled with taking it into his own hands. He still craved his mark, significance, or calling. He loved movies like *Gran Torino* with Clint Eastwood. He thought that would be the most amazing way to exit the world! I will never forget when our daughter potentially needed emergency kidney surgery as a baby, long before we knew what was lying ahead, and my dad piped up, "Take mine! Not much else of me is worth it, but I have good kidneys and what a legacy to leave with my beautiful Hannah. Bring it on!"

"Settle down, Dad," we said. "Relax. All this will work out."

June 2014 rolled around, and it was time for my nephew, Craig, to graduate from high school. We planned a trip to Castlegar to join the celebration. Our family loves to gather around good food, music, laughter, and games. By that time, Dad would take a seat in a surrounding chair and doze off amidst all the chaos and fun. But he managed to dress sharply and muster the strength to act as a cheerleader for his grandson, whom he was so proud of, and participate fully in Craig's graduation.

As the day ended, Dad pulled me aside and asked to speak to my family in the truck out front before we headed back home. We could sense the somberness and compassion in his humble presence, and we all gathered in the truck anticipating his words. My dad used this time to say goodbye. He had tears in his eyes and a peace about him that resonated powerfully as he expressed his deep love for all of us and proceeded to say that because of his children, he had truly lived. He told us all he was so proud of us and would have us in his heart forever. He never said the word "goodbye," but the undertones were truly clear. Soon, we would all embark on a new chapter of our lives.

In July 2014, I felt a prompting to go home on my own, so I hitched a ride with a friend to Castlegar to surprise my parents, something I did from time to time. When I arrived home, Dad was sound asleep on the La-Z-Boy, wearing a "Grumpy" T-shirt and sweatpants. He tried to jump up and greet me, but his stammer and stagger prohibited it. He wanted to go for coffee. (He always wanted to go for coffee.) Quiet resonated amidst our company as we both knew another story was unfolding. I could tell he was retaining fluid over his entire body, and his every step looked like a marathon for him.

I broke down and asked him if I could take him to the emergency room at the Trail hospital. Dad didn't like anything to do with hospitals. He always believed hard work would fix everything—the "no pain, no gain" mindset. He agreed only if we stopped at a Tim Horton's on the way. So, we shared our last cup of coffee together before I took him to the Trail Hospital where he was met with a compassionate team and admitted. He looked up at me from the wheelchair and said with a tone of pure exhaustion, "I will give this another go for you, Spunky." I wrestled with the inevitable.

After numerous scans and tests, the doctors decided Dad suffered from congestive heart failure and they proceeded with the means to clear the fluid from his body so that he could gain some strength back in his heart. There were a few results yet to be shared. My Dad also suffered from colon cancer. His colon had ruptured, and my dad was at the septic stage. Surgery at this time was deemed too risky.

I slipped out of the room to get my dad a coffee. Upon my return, my dad sat at the end of his bed with tears rolling down his face, reciting the poem "Invictus" by Ernest Henley: "Out of the night that covers me, black is the pit from pole to pole, I thank whatever gods may be for my unconquerable soul...I am the master of my fate, I am the captain of my soul."

I listened to him in awe, wonder, and silence deeper than words can grasp. I heard the undertones of Dad preparing to meet his maker. I asked him if he would like me to wheel him outside to see the sunshine and the mountains and he nodded yes. As we found a peaceful place to sit, he shifted his eyes to the mountains. He wore a brilliant mask of wisdom and grace as he spoke prophetically. I proceeded to record with my phone words from a dying man...my dad, James (Jim) Leo Pilla. This is what he said to me:

"If you truly love, you have the power and the strength, and you can stand against anything. You can conquer anything. As much as you let God give you it is always there. You cut His love off by the world—through greed and distraction, by false happiness. You will run and go nowhere. All the time if you open your eyes the beauty of life is right in front of you.

"You are responsible for the circumstances you are in. Community has invested in you. You are the captain and the master of your fate, the captain of your soul. If you see this and believe this, you will have no excuses.

"It takes courage to do the right thing. It demands of you. If people could only see the joy beyond the monetary. Why did God give us the Ten Commandments? Not to give us rules to feel guilty of, or limitations. He gave us them so we would not hurt ourselves and lose freedom. The only force that can withstand the storms of this life is three—the couple (husband and wife or partner) and the strength of Christ in their lives. The foundation of all that is good. To serve others is to know the fullness of this life and to see beauty beyond, and to know the truth of what it means to know joy from within the soul. It demands of you and it requires sacrifice, courage, and responsibility. You have this choice.

"Stop hurting one another, stop chasing the mundane happiness that will always return to you empty—that is this world. Instead, look beyond, reach deeper, and grab on to what is true and good, and the joy you will know will be more than you could ever imagine.

"Pay attention to examples around you and the community that has invested in you. Listen and pay attention. You are responsible for where you are now and where you choose to head. God has created such a beautiful world; it is our human nature that makes it ugly. If we could only see outside of ourselves to serve one another, what is not of this world will reside within us as what I know to be true joy. That's all that matters. That is just all that matters!"

CHAPTER THREE

Oceans Deep

"Remember your leaders who spoke the word of God to you.
Consider the outcome of their way of life and imitate their faith."
—Hebrews 13:7

We had just under three months with my dad before God called him home. He managed to visit our new home in Kelowna and called it "the best last stop before heaven." And on October 28th in the hospice room in Trail, BC, we all gathered—immediate family, all super seven grandchildren, and closest friends—to thank my dad and to bless him with a celebration of his life.

We all shared a toast of Texas tea (aka rum and Coke), and my brother Grant shared some black cherry chocolate yogurt with my dad, his favorite. He was already slipping away. Then later it came time to remove all sources of nourishment so my dad could shut down peacefully from his living presence in this world and move on to his eternal home.

He managed to keep his sense of humor along the way though. Mom, out of respect for Dad's siblings, called the priest to come and give him the last rites. Dad looked at the priest with tolerance, but some surrender as well. As the priest spoke the words, my dad tried to fool us all by holding his breath with us standing by wondering if it was the real deal or would his chest rise again?

While we waited, Dad said clearly, "It sure takes a damn long time to die." This elicited a collective eye roll and laughter among us all.

When the nurse came to adjust his heart monitor stickers on his chest, she had a hard time trying to navigate his copious amounts of chest hair. He said to her, "I descended from the gorilla, but some didn't make it."

Dad liked the word "fantabulous" during his bed bath time too. As a nurse came in to give him a sponge bath, she asked him if his things were in order—if he had a plan for what was coming. Hint, hint. My dad boldly declared, "Absolutely. Off to the crematorium and one last blow." He mimicked blowing ashes from his palm, and the nurse nearly fainted before keeling over with laughter. That was a first for her!

Sometimes when I go through struggles of this sort, I tend to look for the profound moments, seeking God for the connection to the story that is supposed to teach me something about life.

My husband Grant and I felt that the time was drawing near when Dad would pass on, and we felt the girls didn't need to stick around for his final breath. They had a final snuggle, exchanged loving words and goodbyes, and then we encouraged them to go back to Grandma's for the night. While my husband was driving them back to their grandmother's, a deer jumped out onto the road, a normal occasion in Kootenay Country, but typically the graceful animals bound across the road and head for the trees.

But this unusual night, the deer jumped to the middle of the road and kept walking in front of their vehicle. Grant and the girls watched, anticipating its next move. The deer continued to lead them and glanced back periodically, like it was checking in. For the final five miles, the deer ended up guiding them all the way home to the base of the hill to Grandma's house. The whole family felt that Grandpa got them home safely for the last time. We agreed it was the sign we were desperately seeking. It confirmed that profound connection we had hoped for. God uses whatever He chooses to meet us on the path and point us back to Him. Grant, Hannah, and Madison felt God that day and knew Grandpa was soon to enter Heaven.

No one ever prepared me for the next part of the story, sitting beside someone as they entered their next life. I wasn't prepared for the sound of the death rattle breathing patterns, nor the aroma of old blood sifting through the air. I will never forget those moments. The fighter in my dad strived to hang on as long as he could. It was growing late, so we all had our moments with him. The midnight hour passed, and I leaned into him with my hand on his heart and my head on his shoulder. I told him it would be okay for him to go be with Jesus and that everything would be all right. He opened his eyes to look at us all one last time and squeezed my finger. Then his eyes looked off in the distance with great anticipation, and he left the room, leaving behind a body filled with cancer and sickness. We knew his spirit had been set free.

The day had come when my biggest fear shared space with me. I could do nothing, say nothing, or make anything happen to bring him back. What would life look like without him? Would I remember all he taught me? How would holidays and special occasions look like now? Who would fill the gap he left behind?

After we celebrated his life and told his amazing story for those who gathered, the busyness calmed, the family headed back to life routines, and all became quiet again. Now it was just me and God and this new way of living in the world. I recall attending church on Sunday and the song "Oceans" was sung by the worship team. Tears poured from my eyes as I cried out to God, "I need to know God that you have my dad and that he is joyful!" That was my heart, that was my prayer; life in his body for the last seven years was misery. Cancer and heart failure were bad enough, but depression is a silent death that traps and confines people to small places, limiting freedom and passion. I did not want my dad back here on earth suffering like he had, but I did want to know that he finally found joy with Jesus. I needed that confirmation.

Following the church service that day, an unassuming person that I hardly knew approached me and asked if I had a moment to speak with her. I did. She proceeded to tell me it was out of her character to share what she had to say, and she recommended that I pray about her experience. She told me that she felt an overwhelming presence of God during the song "Oceans" and sensed a spirit of deep love. Then she continued to tell me that God asked her to tell me that "He's got my dad, and he is joyful!" Stunned silence enveloped the moment. The Creator of the universe heard the cry of my heart in a small church in Kelowna, and through a woman that God loved, He wanted to bless me with an answer to my prayer!

Devastating love that went far beyond the scope of my mind to even understand was poured into me through that miracle. It gave me the great gift of peace, and my personal grief journey for my dad changed course that day and has offered me something more substantial—a different kind of story for me to choose to pay attention to.

CHAPTER FOUR

———————

Sparkle

*The very soil we loathe may be capable
of producing the crop we most desperately need.*
—Unknown

Now that I'm in my forties, it is evident to me that I spend as much time learning new things as I do unlearning patterns, habits, and behaviors that I've acquired through my family of origin, culture, experience, and from those who have influenced me.

I also realize that multiple things can be true about us at any one time, and it is a healthy journey to wrestle with God in understanding who I am, how He has designed me, and how He plans to fulfill His purpose through me, calling out of me possibility, potential, and purpose. I feel my forties mark a season of discovery about my own unique identity through forming my own words to express my inner thoughts and desires, instead of quoting people much smarter than me.

I also find myself thinking more about how I think, checking in with the inner alignment of my values and how they are expressing themselves as I act on them. As I move through life's opportunities, I have a clearer sense of my orientation. I call it vertical or primary orientation. A direct line to Jesus comes first, and then I'm open to His grace through the relationships He has woven into my life and the community that informs my growth and shaping.

I realize more and more that I will only be fully alive and fulfilled through my relationship with Jesus and others, and it is through God's grace being channeled within these interactions that helps me to see the person that Jesus sees in me. Even if some of these relationships are painful and challenging, I trust that God will use them in powerful ways in my life.

I find my attitude to be more intentional in my efforts to own my influence in ways that inform others of their potential. I try to take hold of the powerful phrase I gained this past year from the Mosaic Conference 2018, which says, "Heaven on earth is doing life with you." Doing life with other people challenges me to consider how I bring peace, unity, and compassion within my circles. How do I contribute to this heaven on earth mindset, or how do I hinder the power that is available to those that do? I realize more than ever we must figure this out. We need to take our focus off the things that divide us, make us feel small, and create an "us" and "them" mindset. In my life, I believe that God uses the curriculum of pain, beauty, and awe to teach us more about this idea of heaven on earth. Still, I fail in some of these divisive areas, especially when I am more focused on myself rather than on God and others. I run out of Wendy power.

The grief path is unique to each person walking it. I believe grief is always with us when our loved ones die. It just manifests in different ways and expresses itself through life in spontaneous connections to that familiar story. Reflecting on the passing of my dad often brings me to that same question: What am I still learning from him and the life he lived? I share with my dad some false beliefs about God and the church.

I have struggled and suffered with a rare autoimmune disease most of my life. It's known as Klippel Trenaunay Weber Syndrome (KTWS) a rare congenital disorder that involves abnormal development of blood vessels, soft tissues, bones, and the lymphatic system. These abnormalities grow around my sciatic and femoral nerve, causing chronic neuropathy and hinders my strength and movement. Two lies that I chose to believe, mostly unaware of those lies until later in my life are as follows:

- **My pain doesn't matter that much; there are others who need God more than me.**

This lie was reinforced mainly because I look physically healthy. Yes, God made me strong, gave me an outgoing personality, and topped it with blonde crazy hair and an imagination that always seems to activate my hope and perseverance when my world shrinks with chronic pain. This outward posture of mine makes my story, most often, unbelievable to others, thus discrediting my expression of pain. I am inhibited from putting in place the boundaries I need to allow for my body to heal, or rest. This disbelief makes it hard to share my authentic place with this pain journey of mine, thus creating a lonely place and voices in my head that defeat, discourage, and often silence my story. Or it makes me exhausted with having the same problem over long periods of time. One of the sayings I am known for among my friends is "pick a new problem." So, I get bored of trying to make my condition believable to others, which has resulted in me finding new stories, engaging in those experiences to quiet the other undermining pain story that feels like the biggest run-on sentence ever.

- **The other lie I continue to fight is that God is punishing me for something I have not asked him to forgive or for a neglected amends.**

No amount of penance list of prayers worked to relieve my pain. There are many religions that reinforce the image of a punishing, Old Testament God—one who demands perfection from you. I have witnessed many people receive healing from God in my life, growing their faith and making them a witness for a miracle-making God that is alive today and available to all of us. People have prayed for me since I was six years old to heal this rare disorder. I am forty-nine today and still suffer with this thorn in my flesh. One of the tensions in this evidence is the question of "Why?" It is a haunting question and a distracting question. Where is that miracle healing from God in my life? So often I stay embedded in my passions, renewing my thoughts with dreams and visions of an exciting life and legacy, distracting the conversations about the pain and many circulating doubts or questions that can fill my mind.

Many people learn to understand later in life that clowns often take on that role to hide hidden hurts in their lives that they cannot control or make public in a safe and meaningful way. It is assumed that many stand-up comics or clowns share this state of being. Robin Williams may be one example.

He suffered from a depressive roller-coaster life. Robin may have been one of those people who believed the lies and hid behind the mask of comedy. He created an identity of acceptance in a culture that fears what they don't understand and is often too busy and distracted to deeply notice another's pain. Sometimes our culture struggles to invest in a person, intentionally and patiently over time, helping bear the burden of such mysterious suffering. This societal dilemma saddens me, and I wish stories like Robin's had better endings than suicide to stop the pain. I hope to learn from him and many others I have witnessed about this tragic ending of life.

I took on the role of Sparkle the clown, dressing up for all family events, fun fairs at school, making people smile, designing balloon animals and balloon swords for the kids, face painting the masks that each person identified with like Superman, butterflies, or rainbows. The children would walk so proudly and confidently with their new faces.

Dressing up as a clown gave me a new focus other than the pain. It hid the story that was going on inside and distracted me for a while, making me laugh and bringing some value to the world with joy and fun. I even went as far to build a tickle trunk of party favorites, running birthday parties for little children from "mad scientist" to "fairy godmother" and back to the familiar party clown. My Sparkle identity brought me great joy. I love children and have always worked with them as a schoolteacher or a daycare provider.

Children always draw me back to the wonder of God and the innocence of life, a refreshing perspective to connect with within my soul. Children trust, they are open to new experiences, they bounce back, they love unconditionally, they are inclusive, and they share openly and ask bold questions fearlessly. I believe now as I look back that these children represented for me the image of God that I preferred to believe in—the image that I sought after and craved in the innermost places of my struggles. I was chasing after the nature of God that I craved so much when life didn't make sense.

I didn't like this religious God who was painted by other people's perceptions and their own lack of knowledge and wisdom. But still, those people had an influence on my life. I not only embedded myself in a child's world, but I also made rescued pets a passion and adopted many from the local SPCA or out of unfortunate circumstances. These furry little friends also served to distract me or create new stories in my mind and even to identify with my pain. There is a reason that dogs are called dogs. Dog is God spelled backward, someone once said. They offer a loving presence always, a quiet strength and intuition into your very soul about how to be "with" you. Dogs seem to have a supernatural instinct that identifies deeply with our existence, and they are faithful over time and circumstance.

My family often jokes about our codependent dog Tucker, a little Havanese Lhasa Apso we have now. He is a cream-colored fur ball with a perfectly shaped caramel heart patch on his side, branded specifically for our family. Our daughter, Hannah, searched him out on the Internet after we lost our other dog, Charlie. Her dad provided a protocol if we were to get another pet, and she mastered it in this little find. I never saw my husband write a check quicker than the day we met Tucker.

He makes us look like we know what we are doing in mastering dog training. He never requires a leash as he owns his spot right beside us and will not waiver, except maybe a little bolt to chase a squirrel. He sleeps right beside the bed, waits patiently at the door to gesture the need to go out or come back in, and even has the discretion to do his business in the off-beaten track, making clean up easy.

Tucker stares at us with his little brown eyes when he hopes to taste whatever it is we're eating, and he brings his toy right to our chests if he feels like chasing his weasel, floppy, or ball. When we are away, he guards our home like a little soldier, paying attention to every sound, waiting as long as it takes to meet our arrival home. He shakes and yelps with excitement. Tucker's whole body dances in all directions every time we walk in the door, even if we only venture out to put the garbage away.

Tucker also has his little attitude, often exuding his alter ego of a Great Dane, owning his turf and staying loyal to his tribe only. He has little interest in widening his circle of human or furry friends, preferring our company. His looks are deceiving. Tucker has such a cute, puppy face that everyone melts when they see him and want to approach him to share some love. Much to their surprise, a growling undertone of disapproval meets them and Tucker retreats to a comfortable distance.

This is such a struggle for me as I know that the general assumption is that dogs resemble their owners, hence I owned two retrievers before Tucker. I always feel so bad with Tucker's abrupt rejection that I find myself explaining his abusive upbringing and his trust issues to everyone we encounter. It has become a bit of an ongoing joke in our family that maybe I need to go to counseling to accept Tucker the way he is. I always feel the need to justify him so others don't feel bad or hurt. Seriously? When I think of it though, it is awesome to be "the one" that gets picked to be loved without distraction or influence from anything or anyone. He makes me smile, and I can't imagine the day when the sound of his little feet will grow quiet. It makes me wonder how my company feels to God.

I also find myself engaging once again in the expressive arts, painting my imagination onto a canvas. I recall my grade twelve art class and the joy I gained from sketching and exploring with different mediums, connecting to my life without words, and how much I loved it. I also remember coloring as a break from studying at university. I found it calming, centering, and a distraction from the ongoing repetition of facts and theories rolling through my mind. I missed that.

About this time, I learned of a ministry offered in our church called SoAP, otherwise known as the South Art Project. I went to check it out. I was greeted by Heather and Maureen, the heart and soul behind the space provided, who invited people to come and play, connect with their imaginations, and explore their stories through different means of expression. I eagerly jumped in and felt that painting would be the best place to start.

I dabbled with watercolors for a brief time, and as I reflect on it now, I realize I was entering this creative space with an ideal in my mind of the result I wanted. I was concerned about wasting any resources. I was impatient with a process that took too long, and I had an inner gauge that drove me to prove that taking time apart from my responsibilities was substantially ineffective. I wanted to turn over completed and perfect masterpieces within the window of time that I set apart every Friday. This set a tempo within me, distracted me from the community around me, and made this more of a competition within myself than a relaxing time of exploring my own expression through art. What a piece of work I was!

Over time I began to understand why I felt the desire to explore this creative mindset. I began to accept the idea of process and the joy of the journey. It helped me to reconnect with my soul through the inspiration that came through color on a canvas, the subtle surprises of beauty that came from my screwups and working past my ideal outcome to accept what resulted.

I noticed that everything around me became an inspiration, from the anticipation of going on Friday mornings, to the drive there, to the words and materials around the room, to the colors and images in my space, to the awakening of creativity among all who participated. I began to anticipate surprise because I had the confidence to step into the space of reigniting my creativity. I found that my creations reflected the parts of my soul that needed to be illustrated whether through silly images, crazy color, or a splash of metallic.

I observed that the whole day would go by while I was lost in time, immersed in my dance with my blobby gobs of paint and my brush—the sounds, the patterns, and the prints it left behind. I felt like the room was a limitless playground. I connected with my childlike wonder, experimenting, making a mess, laughing, moving closer, standing back upon request from Heather and Maureen, gaining perspective of what is or what could be.

I invited texture and tools, a favorite being the putty knife now, that were unfamiliar, like the dowel, unleashing elements of possibility and wonder. I further noticed my pain retreated to the background. The world of smallness and hiddenness disappeared with every stroke. I was beginning to package my pain and struggle into beautiful expressions of abstract color and design.

The colors of silver and gold needed to be added to every picture in my mind, bringing forth the cherished treasure of my own soul. God intended the expression to come alive in its own uniqueness and form. My story no longer feels like a run-on sentence, but rather a portrait of beauty captured in every moment and expressed through my blobs of paint smeared with putty knives. I felt and still feel a deeper connection to the Master Artist. God, the creator of all wonder and beauty, has invited me into this place of joy with Him.

2 Corinthians: 5-17 reads, "Therefore, if anyone is in Christ, he is a new creation; the old has gone, the new has come."

My friend, Jane, has been boldly overcoming cancer these last few years, drawing all who know her into an unfamiliar pain. We can't completely identify, but she allows us to witness the raw and real struggle with this disease and the power of her faith in Jesus as she claims life in Him. Jane received a prophetic word from one of her soul friends during a difficult path of treatment, and she hadn't yet shared that word with me.

At the time, I was staring at a large, blank canvas, imagining the bulldog I wanted to bring to life. You see, I've always had a love for bulldogs and wiener dogs. They make me laugh until my stomach hurts. They have such great personalities, and they occupy a big space for such a small presence. I honestly drop to the ground and greet every available one I encounter on my excursions, often finding photos in my albums recalling the precious moments along the way.

One day, I had the studio all to myself. When I put my canvas on my easel, sporting my painting smock, I began the dance. "Tank" came to life. I laughed, I played, I built his personality through abstract texture and shades, creating this life-size presence that demanded some attention.

After I finished the painting, I took him home, but we have little space on our walls to mount a canvas this large. But I wanted to put it up anyway to see if my family would notice him when they came home. I hung it on a wall where at least a quarter of the print hung over the edge. I proceeded to make dinner with Tank in my peripheral vision, giggling a little...almost like he was alive and living with me. I was always tempted to get one, but the voice of reason pointed to the endless stream of drool and their short lifespans, thus curbing my desire.

Personally, I feel my family would envy the time I spent with such a dog. When my husband Grant got home from work, I alluded to my precious creation. He took a step back and said, "Now that is a big "f@#$'n" dog!"

What! I rarely hear that kind of language come from him, but we laughed so hard because Tank was truly a life-size bulldog invading our home and demanding our attention. So, as you can imagine, the new title of the painting became "Big F@#$'n Dog," prompting me now to imagine a whole series of big "f" things.

Later that evening, I received a text from Jane inviting me for coffee the next day. I accepted. As we chatted over our coffees, our conversation took flight. She shared with me the prophetic word her friend had spoken over her. Her friend compared Jane's journey to a bulldog kind of strength, and God would provide the grit and substance to heal. Jane then asked me if I could look for a picture or painting of a bulldog because she felt it would bring her hope and inspiration as she spent some serious hours resting and restoring her health in a confined space. I knew exactly where to find one! Who knew God would use my playtime and creativity in such a way?

All my life, challenged by this pain, I find myself constantly seeking after the nature and presence of a compassionate God. I crave connecting to something more, and I am finding it in the opportunities and people He has given me. I must look at it all a little differently, shifting my perspective, allowing the power of God's Spirit to take me beyond the limitations of my circumstances.

Through my clowning, rescuing dogs, and creating, my trust in Him is built. Even if my pain remains, my strength is renewed. I want to fly, and I want to run and not grow faint. In the Scriptures, Paul continues to inspire me in his barbaric and almost crazy nature. As we read the bible, we learn that Paul always had a "thorn in his flesh." We are not totally sure what it was, but we can make some assumptions or draw some conclusions, but the most important thing for me to grab hold of in his story is that his suffering made the gospel known fearlessly in his circle of influence through the ages.

I was recently given a book written by Scott Shaum called *Uninvited Companion* that shared a different perspective with me. Scott alludes to these places of struggle, stating that all the challenges can and will offer something more substantial in our lives if we just choose to trust what we don't know yet! I am choosing to trust what I don't know yet.

In the meantime, I am still practicing what James's letter in the bible invites me to consider: "Consider it pure joy, my brothers and sisters, whenever you face trials of many kinds because you know that the testing of your faith produces perseverance. Let perseverance finish its work so that you may be mature and complete, not lacking anything." —James 1: 2-4.

So here I sit contemplating the "why" of my perceived unanswered prayer, and it brings me to an understanding for this time in my life that in this circumstance God has brought me to the end of Wendy. I can't do anything more to make myself healed with the resources presented to date. I have brought my loaves and fishes to the situation. But my understanding from Scripture is that I am to bring all I have, anticipating the miracle—the mystery of what I desperately want to believe but still can't see.

I believe I am now in miracle territory, where my real life intersects with the divine. Where Scott Shaum would allude to as the scope of what I know is stretched past my personal experience, increasing my understanding of what is possible through a magnificent God. There is a peace within me now that is harder to articulate, but it requires from me less struggle than with my question of "why?" It also gives me more strength to believe in the life God has in store for those who believe in Him. I am in a trusting place with God and this pain thing. I even feel I have a solid recipe for my chronic pain shifting my self-talk from the "Why won't he heal me?" to "How can I live joyfully with it?" Thank you to Scott for helping me reframe this mental shift.

I also have discovered that God used the very things that I judged or rejected to bring me a different kind of healing and to this new understanding of Him. So, I offer you my recipe for chronic pain management.

My recipe for chronic pain management goes like this: First, get re-amazed by God! Find that thing that inspires you, that ignites your imagination, that gives you life and energy and then immerse yourself there. For me, I pray the Scriptures and journal the thoughts that emerge from those places, finding new hope and revelation over time. I take these revelations to my painting, to go on life-giving adventures, to meet new faces, or to hold babies or puppies. My life is so much richer and less pain filled when I leap with faith into a new venture.

I will never forget the year my dad passed away. I ventured to the Island of Loretto with my soul friend Louise. We joined a group of others from Portland on this catamaran to explore a natural eco-wildlife reserve on the coast of the island. It was a beautiful day—blue sky, sunshine, new friends, and the ocean awaiting our sail. As we skimmed the surface of the calm water, I found myself thanking God for the time away, surrounded by the mystical waters, jagged rock formations, the warmth of the sun, and new friends to share the adventure with.

I proceeded to ask Him if he would let me see one dolphin as I held onto the memory of my dad like I was feeling him in the air. Moments later the water shifted and out jumped what seemed like hundreds of dolphins surrounding our catamaran, swimming under, leaping over, and playing like they had found a freedom. They splashed us like children and drew us near to this energy that I've never sensed before. We were uplifted by the presence of such beauty, and we all leaned over to touch the dolphins and to feel the spray of the water.

Shortly after, manta rays joined the dance of the dolphins, spreading their fins, capturing whispers of the wind that held them in flight for enough time to imprint them forever in our minds. Then they blanketed the ocean surface with a boom. What an unforgettable gift! What a perspective to grab hold of forever. One dolphin would have been cool and an answer to my prayer, but an entire pod is purely majestic. God spoke to my heart, showing what he has in store for me!

Second in my chronic pain recipe is to hang out with someone worse off than you and gain some perspective on your struggle. I have so many friends who give me perspective. My friend, Heather, knits beautiful sweaters as Parkinson's disease robs her of movement and freedom.

Lauren's syndrome (Prader-Willi Syndrome) causes children with this disorder to endure constant hunger. They are intellectually impaired and have many behavioral challenges. These problems make it difficult for Lauren to widen her circle of friends and caregivers. Therefore, she is easily dismissed by caregivers. She can't always make the connection with her ongoing, roaring starvation and her empathy for others, creating a lonely place and a constant fight for her family to receive help.

I also work at NOW Canada, a society that serves exploited and vulnerable women who suffer from various addictions, mental and physical health challenges, and the ripple effect of fear and violence. Here, I find beauty and strength in the unknown places and crave to love them, facilitating a process that helps me identify with more than their worst experience.

Thirdly, is to volunteer wherever you can! Get outside of yourself and bring life to someone or something else. Something profound happens in the soul when you sacrifice your time. Our family is taking a trip to Africa in a few weeks to work and serve in a developing village called Bogani in Kenya. We will also safari our way through the wildebeest with the Maasai warriors. I will add that story when I return, prepping our imagination for what's to come later in my book.

Richard Rohr alludes to volunteering/serving, when he writes, "At one time this type of service was mostly an act of faith, but now we have evidence to back it up: serving others is a healing balm to our own souls."

Finally, create something, explore expressive means to awaken to something more substantial, tell yourself a different kind of story, dance, paint, write, do anything that refuses to shrink back and isolate, disconnecting from your authentic place and the Creator himself. Connect to something good, life-giving, truthful, or noble. When we choose to step into who we are in Christ, it is liberating for ourselves and for those who are watching us. Your time is now!

Look at Captain Tom Moore, the war veteran, who completed 100 laps of his Bedfordshire garden by his 100th birthday, receiving support from more than 1.5 million people during the Covid-19 pandemic, raising almost 33 million pounds for the National Health Service. Now that is quite a substantial legacy. What a great way to celebrate 100 years of life!

Steven Furtick once wrote, "Your wounds of this year will not be your weakness in the next, BUT the windows through which God shows His strength."

I am honored to have been given permission to share this poem written by a cherished friend of mine who was very instrumental in shifting my thinking about the healing of the creative arts.

An invitation to create by my artisan friend Heather Parlane:

Imagio Dei—Get Gooey!

I've heard your plaintive cries,
the repetitive reel of old standby's,
that echo throughout,
the would-be-creatives of this race.

'I don't have an artistic bone in my body!'
'I can only draw stick men.'
'My wife makes all the design decisions.'
'The only thing I paint are the walls.'
'I suck at drawing!'

'I used to do art...'
But, I also hear parents daring just a bit,
as they view their children's art.
'Oh! That's so beautiful, so fun!'
'I would like to do that.'

'But, I've outgrown play.'
'I'm embarrassed by my simple images.'
'I learned ways to stay away from,
gooey-things.'
'I've grown up.'
'I've forgotten how to be curious,
to take risks.'

Fear not!
You're right.
You don't have an artistic bone,
in your body!
Trust me; bones have nothing to do with it.
But creativity lives within us,
within all of us.
As beloved Brene, so beautifully states:
'The only unique contribution,
we will make to this world, will be born of creativity."

Whatever form your creativity takes,
you were made,
in the image and likeness of God.
In the image of God
made to love, imagine, and create.
In the likeness of God
made with a desire to be more like Him.

So, consider the lilies of the field.
Awaken to something fresh and new,
an expression of wonder and joy.
Reclaim something once lost.
Allow ourselves to play,
and perhaps,
even give some beauty back.

There is a mystery in working with
our hands, our head, our heart.
A chance to visit our feelings, our values, and walk tenderly in
community.

Discover your strong voice, a call to action,
born through the potent force of creativity.

So, if you'd like a place to start,
to experiment and rediscover,
there is a place not quite like any other.
Beyond those doors, open to all.
A place to give and take,
be solo, be communal,
learn and make mistakes.
A place for stick men,
to paint on the walls,
to take risks and get gooey!
Or, perhaps just to sit,
silently allowing the process of creating,
to remind you, of who it was,
who made you.

CHAPTER FIVE

Roof Crashers

"The oak fought the wind and was broken,
the willow bent when it must and survived."
—Robert Jordan

I often refer to the story in the gospel of Matthew where a crippled man, yet to be healed from his pain and suffering, had a few buddies who believed their faith was enough. This story unfolds thousands of years ago when first world conveniences and privilege were not a way of life. Any excursion required lots of time, planning, courage, faith, and perseverance, especially in this case.

During this time, Jesus was teaching and healing, drawing crowds wherever he went. Friends of the paralytic decided they needed to make this risky journey for their friend to carry the burden of his illness to Jesus, the one sure place for those who struggled. There was no room even at the back of the building when they arrived. Crowds surrounded them, and all were keenly focused on this amazing teacher.

So, the men considered another way to get their paralytic friend to the Healer. They climbed up on the roof of the building, carrying their friend, and dug their way through the roof to lower their friend to the feet of Jesus, the ultimate healing source.

The friends carried him to the location, lifted him to the roof, dug away the clay and straw and whatever else the roof was made of, and then lowered their friend to Jesus. Where was the crowd raising havoc over the shock of such an entrance or the damage caused?

I wonder how the paralytic's friends would have felt if no one had been there when they arrived, since timing would be so unpredictable in those days. What if the entire roof gave way from all the weight and digging? So many things could have gone wrong for his friends. I don't know if I would have even started the journey, calculating all the "could haves" beforehand. I probably would have resorted to my all too familiar thinking, boxing God into my limited scope of the circumstances. I also considered how I might have underestimated the power of the faith of my friends.

Years ago, I started this study called "The Journey," through Vantage Point 3—a deeper journey into discovering who I am, who God is, and what He intends to do through my life. This formation process inspired and challenged me alike. Not only does the content continue to stretch and grow me, but the unlikely crew who gathered with me was one of my biggest surprises. It was an all-women's group, a typical recipe for disaster in my experience. I prayed about the group who would study alongside me and share the insights and deep questions that emerged from our discussions. Only seven women participated. Little did I know then about the healing that would happen in my soul among the widely held assumptions that I carried so raw and real about the danger of trusting women. Little did I know how their faith would bring healing in my life.

One question from VP3 material that I recall was "What is it like to be on the other side of me?" That got me thinking of so many things like, what kind of wife am I? What kind of mom am I? What kind of friend am I? How does my influence affect others?

I braved these roundtable discussions with a few inner circle people, and it encouraged me to consider my intentions and actions in relationships past and present. This took a significant amount of time, discipline, humble reflection, and confession. Did I measure up to this idea of a "roof crasher" type of person?

You see, some of my talents—strengths if you will—are motivated by momentum, results, and outcomes, creating an expectation that I can impose on other people. Sometimes, I'm not even aware of what I'm doing. This revelation led me to challenge myself. As I read, prayed, journaled, and shared in meaningful discussion with this women's group, I began to hear a gentle voice saying, "Wendy, you are not responsible to change people. Trust me with how I have created you to influence others. Orient your life to my ways. Let go of gauging your success through others."

"Wendy, I am the only fixer. It is only through me that people will find truth, hope, and ultimate freedom; my yoke is easy, and my burden is light. If you choose to see these women as my children and focus on all that is good in them, there will be strength from that unity. Wendy, unity is the word I have for you. Am I enough for you? I love you because you are my daughter. Come and just be with me."

In case you're wondering, I never hear an audible voice from God with these direct statements, I hear these thoughts form as I read Scripture, pray, listen to a podcast, or reflect on my own personal growth. I write them down because they help me make sense of my own personality and how it affects my interactions with others and with God.

After much prayer and reflection, I decided, through the roof-crasher inspiration, that I would practice some of these unfamiliar qualities intentionally in my friendships. I would look for ways to unburden, consider a different way when needed, and to point my friends back to Jesus wherever I could. I invited a few people into this walk of intention with me and thought it would make for great coffee conversation as we went along. Little did I know that God invited an entirely different group of women to shape me even more, which I will share a little further on.

I asked these few friends to speak about my talents and gifts and to encourage more from me in my spiritual growth so I could reach my God-given potential. I then declared that I would practice walking out some of this within the context of our relationships, leaving room for grace and honest feedback. I think this was the day I declared war on myself.

I thoughtfully considered a friend whom I really enjoyed spending time with during this chapter of my life. For anonymity's sake, we will give her the name "Amiga." My friend, currently, was in a community group with me, and we were building outreach within our group working with local churches to support a low-barrier women's shelter in dire need of upgrades. Each week, we were challenged to create awareness and invite responses to our project.

We had limited resources and a community of churches that was a bit cautious to partner with us due to the economic recession. There was also the stigma surrounding mental health and addiction issues that sometimes discourage people from giving. Our shelter hosted many women suffering from addiction, mental health problems, and trauma. Sometimes these types of issues are not understood, so it shuts down the courage to reach out and help.

We worked alongside many women who faced both challenges and victories in the process, ultimately completing the shelter renovation. Little did I realize that God was not only helping us fix this building, but He was also divinely renovating my heart.

During this time, my friendship with Amiga grew richer, and the power of community working collectively to create something bigger than ourselves resonated in each one of us. By taking on an element of risk with others and following through, we built trust and loyalty that is unforgettable.

Amiga and I continued working together, sharing our strengths and talents within various local outreach opportunities. As our friendship grew, we laughed and cried, forming a relationship that was so precious to me. We shared the most vulnerable spaces of our hearts with no judgment, imposition, or assumption. I would never have believed it could happen in women's friendship circles.

We liked the "Roof Crashers" way, leaning into our faith and love of friendship. Over time, she shared with me the challenges she was facing in her marriage. She felt trapped by legalistic shame, which suffocated her relationship with herself, with God, and with her husband. Her heartfelt cry for help moved me deeply as she sought answers and truth.

In and through her difficult situation, I remember Amiga as a friend who would make me laugh until I cried. She would listen to my life story, and whatever my heart spoke, she met me there. When we reached hurdles, struggles, or any victory, we would say to each other, "Meet me at the beach!" We would break away and sit by the water to process life events together, trying to make sense of our heads and hearts in a way that honored who we wanted to be.

One of the most cherished memories with Amiga happened when I was experimenting with another alternative pain management regime. I wasn't really on my game; it made me feel so sick and exhausted. Alone in my house, thinking of all the things I should have been doing, I looked out my window to see my friend and her two little kids carrying baskets and bags toward my house. They entered my home, and she told me not to move as she proceeded to decorate my dining room table, placed a meal on my warm stove, and set freshly baked banana bread in cloth-covered baskets at the center of my table. I was overwhelmed by their love.

I never had a friend deliver me a home-cooked meal on a weekday, while demonstrating such joy in creating the atmosphere and the food for me and my family. She gave me the biggest hug and then carried on with her day. Wow! I had the opportunity to receive love in an unfamiliar way, especially since my self-sufficient mindset told me I didn't need help from anyone. Her gift of hospitality changed my faith in friendship.

I have a roof-crashing friend and that felt like a devastating kind of love. For those who know me well, they will understand how powerfully her generosity affected me. My school years were marked with much pain as I was bullied, like many others were. Later in life, I also trusted and followed the wrong female leader in my professional development. It reinforced my preconceived notions that I was dispensable and unworthy of grace and forgiveness.

I told myself a false story that became hardwired in my relationships with women, building more walls, insecurities, and dangerous assumptions for my well-being. Amiga broke through those barriers, until one day, our friendship came crashing down. I discovered the gripping pain of betrayal deeper than I can even articulate. As a matter of fact, it has taken me four years to even write about it.

Amiga struggled for years with her unhealthy home environment. Her life and marriage generated so much hurt within her that she lost the drive to even navigate her situation. Instead, it created an emptiness and loss of desire to work it out. She grew tired and empty, so I reverted to the "fix-it" Wendy because watching people struggle was so difficult for me.

I invited her to come home with me to visit my family and stay in a little mountaintop B&B, where she could experience small-town love and find a place to quiet all the noise. That journey home changed everything. Amiga betrayed me there and ended up entering and invading some tender places of pain that I rarely shared with anyone in my family. She attempted to rewrite her own story with new people and opportunity.

Sometimes, we search for ideals outside of ourselves instead of taking on the challenge of considering the true source of joy and fulfillment within. I leaned into the difficult conversations with her without success, so a desire was born in me to lean into other broken people. But the distraction didn't fix either me or anyone else. At times, life confronts us, inviting us to work through our pain—to feel it, to identify it, and to reconcile with it. Without that process, we can't take our peaceful vulnerability into the next experience with freedom and a little more strength and wisdom.

Crashing through the roof costs too much at times. Sometimes we just don't understand or have the courage to carry out our crusade to do the right thing in God's eyes. I know that I have my version of this story, experiencing it from a different point of view, knowing also that I placed too much Wendy power in the roof-crasher ideal. The truth is hard sometimes, and nothing in this process or chapter of our friendship aligned with how I was learning to be true to myself and God and how I was to love other people.

Now that time has passed and some of the hurt has healed, we've all gone our own separate directions. Now I find myself thanking Amiga. First, when I think of her, I go back to the best part of our friendship when she sacrificed a little to make a beautiful meal, blessed my home, and taught me to receive help, which oftentimes I struggle with still.

It was also Amiga who inspired our home group to take on the lead team role of the shelter renovation project, which introduced me to incredible women whom I have the honor of gathering with weekly. As I spend time with these women, both young and older, I realize God confronted my assumptions, my divided mindset, and my deepest fears to show me his amazing love. The vulnerability of the untold stories of the NOW Canada community continues to inform my heart about our miracle-working God who delights in and sings over His daughters—all of them!

A woman in leadership at Christian City Church (C3) in Kelowna said the most powerful statement to me at just the right moment. She invited me "to choose not to be offended now, before the thing happens, because one day it ends up funny or it is overcome by a larger challenge." That makes so much sense to me, as ultimately, it is not the person who is offensive, it is the power of the story we are looking for when we are with them. Darkness resides in all of us, and we choose what we pay attention to. What a shift in thinking for me—a life-giving shift!

I realize now that the burden of pain that most people carry should be the very thing that I hold with grace when behaviors try to divide relationships, instead of taking it all so personally. Hurtful behavior is often rooted in something so much deeper than a negative interaction with a person or a one-off circumstance that raises uncomfortable emotions. This challenges me today to consider and contemplate the burden of the hidden stories of others to be much more important than mean outbursts or unfavorable behavior that makes me feel unloved. It is a humble realization that often it is just not about me.

Most importantly now, Amiga opened the door for the opportunity to experience something more substantial, the devastating love of God that carried me through the feelings of betrayal and loss. I never knew this new depth and scope of God's love until then. He is steadfast through the waves and He is gracious when we fall; the words from Josh Leventhal echo through my heart with his song "Steadfast." I think I listened to that worship song a hundred times through that period.

When I thought or told myself over and over that I could have really used that roof crasher, Jesus was my roof crasher. He walked with me through the layered and difficult season of my feelings of betrayal, through the pain of my dad's death going on at the same time, through the sickness of my daughter, and into the beauty of the unknown.

I have a deeper understanding of the story when Jesus told Peter in Matthew 16:18, "and I tell that you are Peter, and on this rock, I will build my church, and the gates of Hades will not overcome it." It is in those places of deep pain, betrayal, fear, and beauty that we venture into the hope Christ gives us. No one else can fill that space. No human roof-crasher, no fairy-tale ending. These places keep drawing us to God's heart and to His miraculous healing potential if we finally learn that life with Him is the answer.

I often joke and tell people that "my inner Pollyanna is slowly dying." I can't look to friends to tap into that kind of God power, but I can tap into forgiveness of self and others and the spirit of unity to receive His power. It takes time to heal and forget, but now I am humbled once again, and I realize a little bit more about how powerful it is to forgive. I am so grateful for that freedom. I am thankful for all the teachers who led me to this understanding, offering me something more substantial in my faith walk.

CHAPTER SIX

The Walk of Honor

Miracles happen every day. Change your perception
of what a miracle is and you'll see them all around you.
—Jon Bon Jovi

I inherited the impatience gene from my dad's side of the family, I am sure. I giggle as I am much more aware of when that trait shows up in my life. I don't have the patience to read instructions for board games or new items that require assembling. That's where my hubby comes in handy. I often joke and say I married my weakness because where my least exists, his best shines. Perfectly matched!

I do like the satisfaction of checking items off the list though. I check off what the day accomplished and create a new one with what is outstanding just to track my progress. I also tend to create a life of many moving parts, so if something is taking too long, I can shift the focus to the more gratifying pace. My family would roll their eyes somewhat in agreement and possibly somewhat in annoyance at these revelations I am sharing.

I like to refer to my last seven years as the wilderness wonder. Yes, it feels like God was motivated to wake me up faster or grow me quicker or take away all I relied on so I would finally just "be still and know." —Psalm 46:10.

Since I last published and had big plans for my first ever book—*Soul Truth, Rekindle the Fire*—my husband quit a potential partnership at a large accounting firm to begin a whole new career in wealth management. Since then, we have moved three times, acquired staff, and had staff leave. We've walked through three major mergers and acquisitions with my husband's work.

At the same time, I transitioned in and out of three new ventures that I thought would be the lifelong dream job. We lost three out of four parents within two years. Two of our golden retriever dogs died, we travelled many parts of the world, including Africa, and we walked our daughter through a major health crisis with a rare kidney anomaly, which she still is vulnerable to. We lost some friends who significantly impacted our lives and learned for now that this chronic pain syndrome (KTWS) I suffer has no specific cure in the world of science. Honestly, it all feels like a bit of a blur, and only now, four years later, do I feel like my spirit has finally come to a state of rest.

I have been somewhat distracted, but I have also been divinely focused for seven years. During this time, I feel as though I have been radically transformed by a love with no bounds that has taken me to a place of deep peace, but also to a place of devastation. I see it as a kind of love that mystifies my soul and draws me in. It's a love that can't be contained and can't be formed through people, but it can only be savored in the "deepest reverence of humanity's mysteries," as someone of influence once said.

Someone also said, "It feels as if I have touched some of the deep and wide majesty of the great I Am." All these moments—struggles if you will—have interrupted my influence, my own personal agenda, and my ever-present checklist, and they have demanded a response from me. Some days within those seven years, I felt that I couldn't get through another day, but somehow there remained a strong force, drawing me, renewing me, increasing my strength, and building my faith. The journey has tested my patience, perseverance, and a hope in the unknown. It has formed a new creation in me—a new story about a living, active God who is just as alive today and more personal than I ever imagined.

Do you ever feel like you're going to burst when you learn something amazing—something that will benefit everyone—and you want so badly for people to hear it, feel it, know it, and crave it? For me it is like a soul "barf"! Pardon my crude language. I just burst with all I have to say, and whomever is in the line of fire gets it all—the big hurl of passion and awakening. Many times, it results in a scary encounter for some. They don't know what to do or think of me. This story is one of those stories that can hardly be contained, a story of a full-circle God, one who begins and ends, and one who always has the last say.

I have always known I wanted children, at least since I was eleven years old. I love kids! I babysat anytime I could, and I knew that one day I would be a teacher and I would have a family of my own. I hoped that my world would be filled with kids. As we all know, our ideals don't always come to pass as we envision, but there is no harm in dreaming about them.

I met my husband at the age of nineteen while attending the University of British Columbia in Vancouver, acquiring my first degree in Human Kinetics. I like to say our story began with the pig and the pirate. There was a pub on campus called the Pit where students would gather to dance and have fun amidst the stress of scholastic demands. A few of my friends and I attended a Halloween party at the Pit one night, and we decided to dress up as the three pigs. Sexy, I know! Well, it didn't take me long to notice this gorgeous pirate across the bar, sporting a tight white T-shirt, displaying his chiseled declaration of the perfect bicep. He was a sculpted master-piece, an athlete of the truest nature, and seemed to be somewhat outgoing. I forgot that the pig attire doesn't always capture the eye of the beholder. He likes to explain it as, "I thought I was seeing triple?" Excuses, excuses. Hence, we didn't meet that night.

Time passed and we crossed paths again, some quite casual, but one rather profound moment. You know...like the kind you see in the movies when the pace slows down, and the wind starts to send a gentle breeze. Eyes lock and embrace as the encounter draws near. Time freezes and fills a space large enough to mark your memory forever and never let you go. That was it; that was us. Then he finally asked me on a date. And here we are twenty-eight years later.

We have much to say about the years of this full circle, infinite God. It is so amazing when you witness answered prayers in a way that you never imagined. Back when I met my husband Grant, otherwise known as Delster or Deli for short, we prayed that God would grow us in the same direction and speak to our lives in ways that we would become closer in Spirit and truth. We never wanted to grow apart in our vision of a fulfilled life.

The career path I embarked on when we were first married was as a teacher at West Point Grey Academy in Vancouver, where I taught kindergarten full time, some primary physical education classes, and coached the school swim team. I was keen to begin my adventure there and found myself spending time in the classroom preparing lesson plans and anticipating the little people I would engage with.

I shared in my previous book the time when one afternoon I was sitting at my desk and I heard a ruckus in the hallway. Much to my surprise, a little man came roaring into my classroom. I wasn't sure how to respond as he quickly glimpsed me and then rushed to explore the items I had organized in the room. Following him shortly after were his parents, who had arrived from Las Vegas for an orientation of the school. They told me they flew in on their private jet for the appointment to start this exciting new chapter in their son Tanner's life.

I admit, I was nervous about the thought of harnessing all of Tanner's enthusiasm, and I hoped they had the wrong classroom. This child made a lot of funky sounds, and he managed to get his hands on everything I had assembled in a matter of minutes. I was praying that he would be in my teaching partner's class. Nice friend! Funny how God works through our disrupters. In hindsight, Tanner ended up being a little angel and one child that plucked my heartstrings very quickly. He was a gentle little person, had a love for animals, and a curiosity that challenged us all. He noticed more than he received credit for, and he really appreciated a good joke or dry sense of humor.

One day I was coaching Tanner in swimming, and he was in monkey mode that day, splashing all over and jumping on my back. Finally, I told him he needed to be careful around my body as I didn't do well with surprise physical encounters. He was one that required explanations for everything, so I showed Tanner my scars and told him that

I have a lot of nerve pain in my legs. He was shocked at the big, long zipper-like scar that extended from my low back to my right foot.

He asked, "What is wrong with you, Mrs. Delcourt?" I told him I wasn't sure what was wrong, but the doctors noticed some things growing in my body that get in the way of my nerves and muscles and cause pain.

Tanner seemed perplexed, and he laughed a little, stating that sometimes people don't always know what's wrong with him either. He proceeded to tell his mom that I had a mysterious problem with my health. You see, Tanner's grandpa, Milan Ilich, was one of the founders of Scottsdale Mayo Clinic in Arizona, a hospital for rare disorders. He was known to help many who suffered from rare diseases and autoimmune disorders, exuding an overwhelming generosity to help people.

When my husband Deli and I chose to spend the rest of our lives together, we both knew the syndrome I have could prevent us from having a family. There were some inherent risks, according to the specialists, so I decided that kindergarten would be a great place to teach where I could love a whole bunch of children like they were my own. If we decided together, Deli and I even spoke about adoption.

The gift I received from the Ilich family sent me to the Mayo Clinic in 1997 to discover the characteristics of my rare syndrome (Klippel Trenaunay Webber with a few funky twists) and to hear that I could have children. It was highly unlikely that they would inherit abnormal overgrowth of soft tissues, bones, vascular malformations, or cystic lesions that interfere with major nerve functions and musculature.

Deli and I were overjoyed, and we welcomed the birth of our first daughter, Hannah, in September 1998. Hannah's birth weight was nine pounds, three ounces, and she seemed to be a strong, healthy baby girl. We chose to name her Hannah because it means "favor or grace." God gave her to us as a gift.

Fast forward seventeen years and we find Hannah screaming in pain and holding her abdomen, requiring an emergency visit to the hospital. We thought she might have kidney stones as the pain came on so abruptly. After a couple of failed attempts to solve her pain and determine her problem in Kelowna, Hannah was referred to British Columbia Children's Hospital in Vancouver.

The head of the nephrology department collaborated with the chief of urology surgery from Vancouver General to discover Hannah had a rare condition. She had a horseshoe-shaped kidney, and there was an extra ureter on one side that was using blood supply from her kidney to keep it thriving. But the extra ureter was not filtering the toxic by-products from her system and had dispensed toxins into her body for years, leaving her septic and terribly ill. The ureter ended up damaging her kidney, too, as it required more blood than what was available.

So, we found ourselves in consultation with the specialists, who asked us for permission to do exploratory surgery on Hannah to resect the damaged part of the kidney and to completely remove the extra ureter. The surgeons would use a new technology—a robot— that would precisely navigate the blood vessels in hopes of avoiding a fatal bleed. This robot would enable an arthroscopic procedure that would prevent the need to cut through layers of musculature, resulting in higher risk of infection and a lengthier healing process for our daughter.

Soon, our scheduled appointment for the pre-surgical consultation to prepare Hannah for what was to come next arrived. Little did we know that one of the requirements for Hannah was that she had to write a living will, stating how her belongings were to be distributed if her surgery was not successful. My heart froze with fear. I never, ever imagined that I would hear this kind of conversation with my seventeen-year-old daughter. Hannah, with a mysterious courage, told the intake nurse with an eye roll that obviously her little sister would want everything, and she completed her thought with a nervous giggle. She also sarcastically concluded that at this stage of her life, she hadn't accumulated much wealth or items to share.

Following our pre-consultation, we were instructed to escort Hannah down to the surgical preparation area. The preparation area equipped Hannah in the proper attire to enter the sanitary surgical zone. Her head covered in a headdress and her body wearing a hospital gown equipped with heater attachments to keep her warm when hot air circulated through, made her look like a Stay Puft Marshmallow. We all got a chuckle out of that. With her little sister faithfully by her side the entire time, we tried to make light of the situation and just enjoy Hannah and keep her calm before she needed to go into surgery.

Out of the corner of my eye, I saw a doctor enter the room. His face was all too familiar to me: Dr. Thomas Zwimpfer, the neurosurgeon, who had performed several surgical procedures on me in my early twenties. One of those surgeries was a result of being misdiagnosed as a potential neurofibromatosis patient. It was strange to stand in his company now with my daughter undergoing exploratory surgery with a rare condition as well.

The time finally came when we walked with Hannah's gurney as far as we could before we had to hand her over to the trusted care of her surgical team. It is hard to express the level of vulnerability we felt when we knew that the coming hours were out of our control.

My husband Grant, my youngest daughter Madison, and I headed to the main floor of Vancouver General Hospital ready to embark on a long, ten-hour journey before we would hear the outcome of Hannah's surgery. We received ongoing texts and phone calls from family and our community, rallying around us with relentless prayer, encouragement, and a willingness to serve in any way that would unburden our family.

We experienced firsthand the faith of our roof-crasher friends and family that included our cherished community of our church back home. Down the corridor, I noticed some art hanging on the wall, so I strolled over to look, and I realized this space was titled the "Walk of Honor." I allowed myself the distraction of taking a little walk to view the beautiful art pieces displayed along the hallway that drew me into a different space.

I then noticed a photo at the end of the walk mounted on the wall. It was a photo of Milan and Maureen Ilich, the family who seventeen years ago gifted me with the trip to the diagnostic Mayo Clinic in

Scottsdale Arizona where I learned that I could have children. The same family, seventeen years later, donated the very robot that was now operating on our Hannah. Once again, the Ilich family provided hope and life to our family. I was rendered speechless, and my body felt like it had just landed in a backward trust fall from a rooftop into the arms of my Savior.

Jesus had known all along how this journey would go. A sense of profound peace covered me, and I fell asleep shortly after to wake up to a successful report from Hannah's surgical team. We then embarked on the road to recovery with our courageous girl. Today, she is doing well as I write this, attending a term of business school at Ecole des Hautes Etudes Commerciales du Nord (EDHEC), in Nice, France—a walk of honor that offered us all something more substantial, a full circle God!!

A Mother's Prayer for Her Sick Daughter

"Heavenly Father, you gifted us with Hannah. You delight in her, you love her, and you care about every detail of her life, and we are so grateful for this. You are calling us out in these circumstances, Lord, making us brave in the upcoming storm. Lord, I pray for a special anointing over our Hannah. I lift her up to you—your power, your healing hands. Shower her, Lord, with your Holy Spirit in an undeniable way. What will Hannah's prayer be? Where will her hope come from? Lord, I trust you with this precious child as you know my heart. My prayer for Hannah is that she be fully restored to spiritual and physical health so she may use her story as salt and light to others who suffer in ways that she has. Give us peace, Lord, in this unknown place; remind us that you are walking ahead of us along this journey. Anoint those, Lord, that will inform her processes. Thank you for Grant, the constant, the steady, the provider, and protector, and for Madi, the sweet little serving heart who notices everything, loves so much, and for her joy-filled spirit and sparkle that brings hope to all who know her. Thank you, Lord, for the community of believers who love and live out what it means to be the body. How humbled we are to be so embraced, so carried, and so connected. Thank

you, Lord, for answering my prayers for a healthy community, for a circle of faith to reconnect, and for all that you give that reminds us of your glory and unchanging nature. I pray before you, Lord, humbly, trusting your lead and the gut sense you've placed within me to respond. I am afraid, and my heart is heavy watching my child suffer. I feel so helpless. Cover me, Lord, as I carry this burden, with the message of your healing power as we wait. I give you my doubts, my frustrations, my urge to yell at people, and I ask you to make me a peaceful agent of grace even as I feel overwhelmed and scared. Reside in me, Holy Spirit; give me that "peace be with you" way of being. Remind me of your scars, Lord, and remind me that you sent Hannah on a journey even if it seems such an unlikely ideal for a mom. I trust you are using this to draw her into the grand narrative and you already know the ending. It is by your power alone that gives us all that we need during this time. Help us learn to use this time to witness you in our lives, and I pray also, Lord, that Hannah's friends love her, and they don't fear the unknown, but they will take this opportunity to grow, to build one another up, and to have hope in an amazing God. In your precious name I pray. Amen.

CHAPTER SEVEN

Baraka

"Umoja ni nguvu" (Swahili for "Unity is strength")
—Wilson Meikuaya

"Asante Sana" (Swahili for "Thank you!")
—Jackson Ntirkana

Recently my family and I traveled to Africa, a dream I held onto for years until the timing came together. I am quite the adventurer and visited almost twenty-five different countries before the age of fifty. But somehow the idea of going to Africa had both a compelling and haunting pull on my heart. I imagined Africa to be a place where I would be re-amazed by God; an experience of awakening I assumed.

Now that I am on the other side of my trip to Africa, still allowing the impact of its influence to sink into my bones, I find myself beyond the scope of my imagination, no easy feat for sure. When I reflect on the majesty of Africa (Kenya and Tanzania), I imagine the sounds of the jungle at night while lying in my tent under a canopy of twinkling diamonds, uninhibited by pollution or progress, drawing me to the wonder of creation. I hear the joyful singing and recall a vision in the distance of a sea of color as the villagers, dressed in brilliance, walked miles to come and meet us and welcome us, dancing, jumping, and holding our hands like we were family members separated by time and experience and finally reunited.

I feel I can improve on my "welcome" back in Canada. I can still hear the children shouting *Jambo* from the distance, see them run toward our truck along the road, white teeth glaring through midnight-black skin, compelling my soul to a deep connection with each one of them.

While there, we waved back until they were no longer in sight. As the days passed, we would anticipate the many Jambo friends along the path of our road trips in and out of the villages. I found it difficult knowing that I had fresh bottled water and snacks packed with me for the day ahead and not be able to share with the children running up to the vehicle. I could have made their day with a huge bottle of fresh water and a snack of fruit and chips.

We were led by WE, an organization focused on global impact projects and collaborating with others to be the change they wish to see in the world. It has been in action for over twenty years and is helping create sustainable, thriving communities in underdeveloped parts of the world by collaborating support and services to build the five pillars of life—health, water, nutrition, education, and opportunity.

The team that escorted us to all these villages challenged me and reminded me that if I were to do that, how would it help that child and the others watching who didn't receive anything? What would happen when that child returned to the village with treasures unheard of? It was a humbling awareness, because it was more about me wanting to do something and feel good about it. I wanted to feel less guilty of the privilege I come from and the many blessings I have each day that many of these villagers may never know.

I was reminded by my new friend, Linda, that the best gift of all is relationship—to hold their hands, to try and connect with a song or a game of football. I learned from WE that the best way to really impact these people was to empower them through education, relationship, and working together toward something sustainable for their culture. Giving them a temporary pleasure of one day with clean water and a snack bought at the store would only serve me.

Her wisdom made me question why I serve in the capacity that I do? I was challenged to reflect on the outreach work I am involved in and questioned the feel-good mindset. I asked myself, is what I participate in making much of me or them? These are good questions for daily personal reflection for me. Now I feel I am aligned well in outreach, so grateful for the reflective practice.

I loved the many early morning, peaceful walks with Maasai warriors, learning about their tribal disciplines, the medicinal qualities of the plants, and the rhythm of life that is so honored among the animals and insects alike. Africa revealed a soul of its own, with its pristine landscape; exotic, yellow-eyed wildcats; prehistoric-looking beasts; and bush babies screaming in the backdrop of fire-like sunsets and sunrises. The gentle warm breeze, the red sand adrift, and seeing miles and miles of wide-open space to run and be free inspired me.

The nighttime stories by the fire, sitting with the last generation of the Maasai warriors equipped with their machetes, kongas, bows and arrows, and sharing the precious songs of their hearts was uplifting. The three warriors—Peter, Wilson, and Jackson warmed by their shukas—shared a time when they embarked on a sacred pilgrimage in honor of their parents and tribal elders. These young men were taught from birth the way of the warrior.

I won't forget one warrior sharing that at the young age of fourteen months, if he cried too much, his parents would make a small cut under his eye so if the tears rolled down his cheeks, they would sting so badly from the salt that he learned to cry no more. A prominent marking of the Maasai warrior is that his two front, bottom teeth had been permanently removed. This resection was to brand the warrior, but it was also helpful when having to administer bitter medicine easily into the mouth.

A young Maasai warrior was the main storyteller the one evening we gathered around a large fire, many of us unaware of what was in store, the vulnerable journey that he would invite us all into. He, in a posture of reverent submission, shared with us how he had become a warrior. He told us that he underwent many challenges to prove his courage and loyalty to family and tribal traditions.

At the age of fourteen and fifteen, he had to go through a series of self-harming activities like burning his own skin without flinching, evidencing the power of the mind in warrior training. At the age of fifteen, he and a few companions were left in a cave, armed with their weapons and nothing else, forced to survive for five months before they returned home. They were on a quest to prove their bravery by slaying a lion. For some, this was the end of their training.

At the age of sixteen, they underwent a ceremony of public circumcision attended by more than two-hundred tribal members. This is a public declaration that the warrior is worthy of the title. Months before this day, however, the father of the warrior in training hangs the knife by the bed, giving the young man time to mentally prepare for what is coming. Often there is a witch doctor or antagonistic tribal member who tries to poison the knife and end the warrior's potential, leaving the warrior in training somewhat paranoid in guarding this butcher knife before the day. It is often the case that the knife is shared and not sanitized, making the young man susceptible to life-threatening infections.

Our storytelling warrior said he prepared his mind and heart for this day because he did not want to bring shame on his village. He went on to share that if he moved a muscle, blinked, twitched, or flinched in any way during this cutting ceremony, the elders found a fattened or pregnant cow and slaughtered it, publicly disgracing the failure and making him a mocked and discounted wanna-be warrior. For all the Maasai in training, the public humiliation of mockery was much worse than the circumcision itself. All three Maasia warriors accompanying us that evening transitioned into notable titles within their tribes and wore their armor proudly as they continued to share the stories of the Maasai.

As these warriors had the opportunity of education in Kenya, they became authors, botanists, and tour guides, interpreting for and guarding visitors as they visit Kenya. They have proved to their families and respective elders that education opens many doors to promising futures, bringing more value than the traditional ceremonies and accumulation of sacred cows. They have transformed minds within the tribes to accept education as the new way of the warrior, and now both men and women have warrior rights through this process of learning.

We were listening to history changing right in front of us and discovering the cost of such freedom for the Maasai. What seemed to them as everyday, honorable living, was nothing short of debauchery and torture in my eyes. I couldn't imagine putting my daughters through mutilation ceremonies, selling them for a hefty dowry and arranging for them husbands they should love for the remainder of their lives.

Gathered around the fire, coming from such different cultures, we shared passions to live strong and fulfilled. I walked with one of the warriors under the stars digging more into this warriorship process, appreciating its deep-rooted loyalty and courage of the human spirit. In the same breath though, I was mortified by their rituals. He laughed at me often, trying to help me reach understanding with encouraging words.

I asked the young Maasai if he had faith. He told me he was a Christian and now believes that God is the way to warriorship, that the body is a temple of His Spirit, and it is no longer a practice of harming to become a warrior. He is married to a wife he chose, and they have a son. He went on to tell me that his son can choose education as the way to warriorship, but what he is learning from his son is that his son wants to be strong and courageous like his dad. I understood from this observation that changing some of these practices will take time. I also left with the haunting thoughts of the extent some people will go to receive approval from a father.

We also visited Bogani Village in Kenya and toured a nearby community where the Kisaruni all-girls school was developed. We had the opportunity to tour the classrooms, meet some teachers, and interact with the students. It was so empowering to hear the passion for learning declared by each student, and the dreams they shared on how they will inform their destinies with faith, hard work, loyalty, and togetherness. The questions they asked us were deep and directed right to the core of our purpose and how our lives will impact the world. The girls set their schedules for school and joyfully awaken at 4:30 a.m. to go to school until 9:00 p.m., six days per week.

They work together to achieve the best results as they know that education is the gateway to success, a sustainable life in their home villages, and the promise of a future much more compelling than the ceremony of circumcision, arranged marriages, and dowry. Even though the young women held tradition and family in high regard, they were determined to inform the generations before and after that there is a better way to live, to love, and to thrive. These girls redefined courage for me.

My family received a special gift when we got to meet Wilter and hear her story. Wilter was twenty-three years old and finishing her university degree in the spring of 2019. She was one of the first girls to graduate from the Kisaruni Girls High School in Kenya. Wilter's story impacted all of us, not just in the circumstances she endured, but for me it was in the posture that she shared it.

In full respect for Wilter and her story, I will provide a small glimpse into how her sharing shifted my life. Wilter was preparing for the traditional practice of circumcision as her fourteenth birthday approached. Her restlessness and inner conflict evidently burdened her because she held her father in a position of honor and was a devoted member of her family. Wilter wanted to respect her parent's wishes and to contribute, but she loved school and learning. At the time, girls were only able to attend middle-school, and then most were circumcised and arranged into marriage for a dowry.

Wilter knew she was smart, and she wanted to continue with school, changing the course of tradition and religious practices within her lineage. Her mom knew her daughter's heart, and when the day arrived for Wilter to proceed with the tribal traditions, her mother asked her, conveniently, to go fetch water from the river. For most women, the water walk could be anywhere from two-to-seven kilometers away from the village. This was a defining moment in Wilter's life because she knew this was her only chance to escape. This was a bold decision since her father was a prominent leader and influential man in the country. Wilter knew he would be on the hunt for her.

But she ran anyway and found refuge from her predestined role by hiding in the jungle for two months with nothing but the courage in her heart, faith in a big God, and the clothes on her back. A fourteen-year-old girl hiding in a wild jungle for two months. I can't imagine.

Wilter didn't dwell on her scary encounters while she told her story. She just skipped ahead to the day she braved appearing by the river and a woman noticed her. This woman changed the course of Wilter's life by taking the young girl into her home to help her heal. She reconnected Wilter to school where she received the top grades in her class.

Finally, Wilter gathered enough strength and courage to return to her family home, bearing gifts and reports on her educational status. Wilter hoped to enlighten her father on a better way for young women, showing him that education would provide much more wealth to a village than a herd of cows. It took some time for Wilter to win over her dad's heart, but eventually she did, and he advocated for women's education in his wide circle of influence. He decided that education could be the way of the warrior in his community in the future.

As you can read, this story is amazing, but the thing that was most profound to me was that Wilter never carried a posture of burden through her story. She never embellished the suffering and torture of the jungle and how close to death she came. Nor did Wilter ever shame or disrespect her father in any way for his traditional practices and disapproval of Wilter's running away, or even the thought of having her own dad hunting her down.

Rather this young African woman spoke only of her passion, the quest she had to go on to reach it, and the heart she had to earn back her father's favor in a new way and new hope for the future. Now Wilter is an education advocate for eighteen thousand other girls pursuing their dreams of being educated, which will lead to a better future for them. She hopes to run her own travel and tourism company one day so many people can visit her country to see how rich in beauty and majesty it truly is. And she is quite interested in politics and plans to be the future President of Kenya. I have no doubt that Wilter will accomplish anything she sets her heart out to do! Her story has filled me with something much more substantial in my understanding of the faith and courage of the human spirit.

Since time has passed and the story of Africa lingers, I discovered a parallel in my life with my new friend Wilter and my mom.

All who meet my mom find her to be classy, very hospitable, and quite funny. If I were to describe her in a few words, I would say she is joyful, free-spirited, and innocently gullible at times.

You see, my mom grew up in an environment that in today's time would alert social services. She was born out of brokenness and ignorance for lack of more socially acceptable words. My grandpa was a tall, slender man, with a simple and kind way of thinking. He was true to his roots of brotherhood, worked hard at his job, and enjoyed the drink and a good game of poker. He was also charming and charismatic in a pair of dancing shoes. Everything else around him seemed to fall into oblivion, including my mom and her sister.

My grandma, a look alike to the notorious Elizabeth Taylor, could even work a room with her beauty at the age of seventy. She enjoyed getting her hair permed; sharing a drink and a good snack; playing a good game of poker; but seemed to fall short of some pivotal self-discovery in my opinion. My grandma's dad left her before the age of ten, leaving her mother as a single parent. My grandma was old enough to believe that men leave, and she was not worth staying for. This led her, in my perception, on a search her entire life, looking for love, significance, dignity, and worth in all the wrong places. A truly sad story really. She numbed her pain at the gaming table and in the drink, leaving the ripple effect of addiction to the vulnerable young girls she brought into the world.

My mom just happened to be a miracle who lived despite all Grandma's unwanted pregnancies. I imagine today that my grandma carried a deep pain beyond her own words until the day God called her home. But my mom had to find a way to live and thrive in these unfortunate circumstances. Out of pure neglect, she learned the lessons of oral hygiene in a difficult way, having all her teeth removed in her teens. She had to pay for anything that she needed or wanted, so the value of a dollar was in her blood. She had guardian angels to protect her when her curiosity got the best of her and potentially dangerous adventures took flight. My mom often returned home to parents who were not in any condition to provide for her needs, leaving her and her sister to tend the home and make meals.

She shared a room with her older sister and even wore her clothes regardless of size differences. She knew no differently. My mom never had a birthday party. She peeked once at a Christmas gift that Safeway allowed her dad to bring home from the annual Christmas party. He was a butcher in the meat department, but because she sneaked a peek, she lost the opportunity to receive it. My mom was offered yummy chocolate bars when Grandma felt a good distraction was necessary. I think my grandmother held a deep desire to give her daughters more than she was capable of.

Yes, I could say that my grandpa gave people the illusion of being somewhat charming. He was filled with one-liners, could enjoy a stack of strawberry waffles with me, and still rip up a dance floor. Pretty much all I recall of him, besides the odd drinking indulgence. My grandma, though always had sadness in her eyes, a sweet smile, and some time to chat with me a little. I paid attention to these two as I never saw many people quite like them. I wondered how it was even possible that my mom came from these two people.

I realize that our families of origin have influence in our lives; they inform our hearts with messages and illustrations of what life should be. We learn to model their behavior, often without even thinking about why we are doing what we are doing. We don't often question authority, especially in those days, as children were simply seen and not heard. I will never forget the time my mom told me that her parents wanted only one child. They told her they never wanted her. I was devastated when my mom shared that with me. I could go on about the dysfunction on many levels in this family dynamic, but I think you are getting the gist of a foundation of brokenness.

Science tells us that secrets create pain and sickness in our lives. It is when we can openly share our struggles, which are different for everyone, that strongholds release their grip and healing happens. When we have the courage to share these tender places, we liberate others to do the same. I wonder how many lives would be saved if we could all be more transparent in our transgressions, sharing the pain with one another, bearing our burdens together with grace and hope.

Much like Wilter, even though her struggle was a third-world condition, my mom shared from her first-world condition. They both had the choice to stay and live in the mindset, the culture, and follow the examples of their parents, or they could take from their roots what they had learned and choose to make a better life, to show a better way, and to ultimately share a different kind of story.

My mom never wallowed in shame about the consequence of her family circumstance. She left home, married my dad, and created an entirely different kind of home for us. We were loved, our home was cared for, our meals were homemade, our birthdays were celebrated, we built treasured traditions around the holidays, we went to church as a family, we prayed as a family, and we worked through our struggles and imperfections with grace for one another. Not perfect by any means, but a whole lot healthier situation than my mom knew as a young girl growing up.

Mom showed all who were watching a different way; she put a stake in the ground when it came to addictions entering our home. She made room at the table for people to join and always left the invitation open to my grandma and grandpa. My mom didn't keep score of their wrongs, but instead she opened a door to something a whole lot more. What they chose to see or learn from my mom later in their lives, I will never know. My mom chose to respond to her shaping opportunities as a child, trusting God with all the brokenness, hurt, and lies, and walked courageously into a new story. She didn't make excuses or shift blame on anyone; she rose above. My mom offered all of us something more substantial. Who knew a parallel from my mom's life and Wilter's life would ever enter my mind? Amazing what our trip to Africa did, and I know it will continue to inform my heart over the years.

I have seen many pictures of Africa's Big Five (the lion, the leopard, the rhino, the African buffalo, and the elephant), amazed at their mysteriousness and wild, but graceful, nature. Nothing quite prepares you for the jungle safari encounters as each one is a surprise and a wonder of its own. When my family flew into the Maasai Mara, en route to Richard's River Camp, we landed on the dirt runways and exited our aircraft right in the middle of the wild game safari. We walked ten feet from the plane and boarded our safari Jeep with our Maasai driver, William, and were instantly driven into the wild.

Three zebras, a grazing giraffe, and an elephant mudding in a nearby puddle greeted us with a chilled posture but an extraordinary beauty that took our breath away. Even on our drives between locations, we were literally on a safari. The animals were free to wander amidst us and beyond, everyone respecting their boundaries and existence, unless, of course, a hungry predator made a kill for sustenance.

We hunted with our eyes and cameras, spotting any movement, and then we drove right up to the edge of its wild existence with only a door separating us from life or death—very exhilarating and slightly frightening in the same breath. We saw a baby giraffe, a half-hour old, stand for the first time, trying to make sense of the awkward imbalance of that exceptionally long neck and four boney limbs.

Our driver approached a lazy lion and lioness basking in the shade under a brush and glaring at us with those piercing, yellow eyes, gauging our motivations before they shared a big yawn and returned to the chill zone. Suddenly, the lioness nudged pappy lion, and he launched to his feet in seconds, shook out his majestic mane, and mounted his mate, creation in the making two feet beside us with some of the most powerful creatures in the world.

No words can quite describe our racing hearts, except that it lasted seven seconds and then the lion returned to nap. We pondered why the male lion was called the "king of the jungle," until we learned afterward that he provides that service fifty to one hundred times per day. No wonder he's tired!

As our thrilling adventure continued, we came across herds of elephants, graceful giants marching across the plains without a sound with their adorable babies in tow, all looking rather leathery and prehistoric. We learned from our guide that when an elephant spots the remaining skull bone after a kill of another elephant, the leader of the herd will walk over to the skull and roll it with its tusk, sniff it, and determine whether it was from the same family. Elephants are known for their incredible memories. After one sniff of us as individuals, they can hold us in their memories for three years. If that elephant skull was the remains of a relative, the entire herd encircles it, embracing the memory and mourning the loss. It was beautiful to watch such a tribute to life amidst the animal kingdom.

At dusk, we still drove further toward the horizon to find two cheetahs nesting on top of a termite mountain, giving them a clear view of their habitat. They didn't seem to mind us sitting only a foot away while we contemplated this cat who can run from zero to sixty-five mph in seconds. Not intimidating at all! I have never held myself in such a posture of respect and humility as I felt on the game ride. After a full-day excursion, we would end our journey with a "sundowner," which included a Tusker Beer, a shuka blanket, roasted nuts, and sharing highlights together of the defining moments on the game drive while the sun went down over the plains. Magical in every way!

We accompanied some of the WE team and their partnering villages to do a water walk with the mammas to work alongside each other to build a girls' dorm at the new university site and to share in the celebration of progress throughout the community. We made instant friends with our coworkers and very quickly became a part of something so much more than we could have ever accomplished on our own. This experience has a way of impacting the soul and forming deep connections through tasks that have no title or prestige, just ones that invite us all to respond with the whole of ourselves, to joyfully serve those less fortunate in opportunity, but certainly not in spirit.

The Kenyans, with their silky, jet-black skin, radiated light that truly transformed our hearts and made divine connections with us that will last forever. I arrived in Africa as one version of Wendy, and through the blessings, or *barakas*, I left Africa shifted in spirit. Now the refined version of Wendy will be changed by this experience for the rest of my life. I have learned more about faith, courage, and what it means to be joyful amidst the struggle.

I have learned what it feels like to be welcomed wholeheartedly, and I hope that I can exude that kind of welcome to those who are in my company. Of course, I don't plan on chasing after cars along the side of the road yelling *Jambo* and waving like a fiend, because in North America I might be arrested. But I sure hope my welcome is reflected in the love I can offer others.

I wrote this chapter en route to Nice, France, accompanying my eldest daughter Hannah as she traveled to study abroad for one term at EDHEC Business School, an opportunity of a lifetime. I sat beside her in the airport waiting to board our next flight, and I asked her what she took away from her experience in Africa.

"Mom, there was most definitely a freedom from judgment and exclusive culture," she replied, "and ultimately, Africa was the biggest culture shock for me because of that."

In a sense, Hannah carried a sadness that the world is missing some of the backdrop of what Africa represents (i.e., a jungle that is wild and free and open versus a concrete jungle of development). The part of Africa that made it so magical for her was the peace amidst the diversity of animals and tribes—an aura of respect and a deep appreciation for the land and its community, doing everything in their power to preserve this gift.

"I will go back for sure one day, Mom," she said.

My youngest daughter had an opportunity to write a final English literature essay for her grade twelve year. She was asked to respond to a question that inquired about a moment in her life that impacted her. Madison responded with these words:

"I keep hearing '*Jambo, Jambo*,' from the kids shouting as their smiles lit up with an immense amount of joy. My heart melted when I came to realize the importance of just a simple wave."

An image engraved in Madison's mind is one she describes as the "rocky terrain, grass waving in the wind, sounds that bring peace to the ears, and not a single worry in the world." She loved to gently place her feet on this "mystical and exotic land, everything seeming to be soothing and calm, as if a weight has been lifted...a giraffe in my peripheral vision, I pinch myself, imagining that this must be a dream."

Little did Madison know that this experience would change her perspective and mentality of life forever. She recalls "grasping on to the leathered hands of the wise feeling a connection stronger than words."

"Mom," Madison said, "the high school students in Africa don't restrict or limit their goals; they adjust their learning to achieve them. I feel Africa believes that we are helping them, but in my perspective, they are the ones rescuing us and showing us the true meaning of appreciating life and taking hold of it."

CHAPTER EIGHT

Wanna-Be-Hero

"A hero is someone who, in spite of weakness, doubt or not always knowing the answers, goes ahead and overcomes anyway."
—Christopher Reeve

I have a young friend named Hope. I met Hope when she was almost five years old when I was teaching backyard swim lessons. Hope is and was an amazing swimmer; she could hold her breath seeming like forever and would live in water if she could.

Hope has Prader Willi Syndrome, a genetic disorder due to loss of function of specific genes. It is a rare condition that causes physical, mental, and behavioral problems. In babies, symptoms include very weak muscles, poor feeding, and slow mental and physical development. A child with this syndrome develops a relentless hunger, which can lead to diabetes or obesity. People with PWS have seven genes on chromosome fifteen that are either deleted or inactive. They will often have low muscle tone, incomplete sexual development, and a chronic state of hunger. They are short of stature, have eyes that might be almond shaped, and their mouths are marked with a turned-down expression.

When I met Hope's parents, I was forever changed. They would qualify as unsung heroes in my story. They exist in the backdrop of everyone's "normal" day, fighting every moment for their daughter to receive education, effective care aids, significant health interventions, and a safe environment to live as a member of society.

Her parents relentlessly advocate for Hope's inclusion, for educating others on the diverse nature of Hope's disorder and trying to create a climate of dignity and worth for their daughter. This is a difficult challenge when the disability itself manifests in undesirable outcomes for people who are not normally exposed to these circumstances. Hope, being in a state of starvation all the time, will grab and gobble food at the sight of it, whether prepared well or not, discarded or unsanitary, posing a threat to Hope's health all the time, but also leaving others on guard in her company.

I am sure you have been what we term as "hangry" from time to time and have gained a minute amount of understanding about the constant state of this for Hope. Understandably, Hope tends to get frustrated and act out with the constant, nagging, and painful irritation of her body, bringing on undesirable results for everyone around her.

I grew to love this family and to quite enjoy Hope. Her parents opened the door to my doing some respite for them during which I would take Hope for periods during the days and weeks, so the family could enjoy their food in the normal way. It gave them a respite from the exhaustive state caused by Hope, who couldn't help herself.

A typical day with Hope would be reading together on my cozy couch, doing a few scholastic activities. Coloring was one of her absolute favorites, especially if it involved cats. We would make a healthy snack together and a cup of herbal tea, then went on a long walk with my dog. On a special day, Hope and I would visit animal shelters, libraries, the bird sanctuary, or go for a drive to a yogurt place for a small treat. My days with Hope were met with success most of the time as she knew what to expect and there were few interruptions to the simple rhythms of life. The times when we met some challenges were when other people were eating a variety of foods in our presence or if other children wanted to interact and direct the activities in an unfamiliar direction. These were all understandable challenges for Hope, and we patiently worked through them together.

One day I was home, and I received a phone call from Hope's mom. She was elated and excited to share some news with me. Hope had been chosen to go on a Wendy's Dream Lift trip to Disneyland!

What? It was a rare occasion for Hope to be chosen for such a special event because her behavior often brought on challenges if anything revolved around food options, new activities that weren't familiar to her, or any kind of overstimulation.

After we shared in the good news, Hope's mom asked me if I wanted to accompany Hope on the Dream Lift as each of the candidates needed a caregiver in charge. I didn't even think it through. I was experiencing the high along with Hope's mom and moved to tears that this young girl might get a break in life and be treated special regardless of her diverse abilities. And who doesn't want to be the hero of the day when the occasion arises? I was ecstatic to have the opportunity to go to the happiest place on earth and to be the super-cool caregiver to Hope in our unforgettable adventure to the enchanted world of Disney.

Hope and I prepared and packed our bags the night before and had to awaken at the ridiculous hour of 4:00 a.m. to arrive at the airport to begin our journey. Her mom also whispered in my ear that there were no restrictions on Hope's diet while we were there as it was only one day, and Disneyland would be filled with treats that would compel Hope's hunger from the minute we arrived.

When we got to the airport, little did we know that a press team would be awaiting our arrival, surrounded by other young, adorable candidates for the Dream Lift. They were all dressed in their Mickey Mouse ears and eager to embark. Little did they realize that kind of attention would elicit no warm response from Hope. She was nothing short of annoyed with people who got in her face, asking her questions about an experience that she hadn't lived yet. Hope always prefers one person to interact with at a time. I gained a slight sense that I had signed up for more than I realized.

All these cute little kids happily sang the Mickey Mouse song, shared their excitement, and performed perfectly for the Dream Lift TV crew. Hope and I hid in the background, while she wore the biggest scowl on her face and mumbled disapproving remarks that created a slight situation of "us vs. them."

Once past the initial hoopla, we headed to TSA security so we could proceed to our gate for the flight. When approached by the security guard, Hope suddenly stopped mid-stride, and in a loud voice, refused to show her hands. She spoke boldly into his direct eye-level that he needed to move because Wendy was taking her to Disneyland. I humbly approached the officer, trying to explain that Hope saw the world differently than security teams in airports, prioritizing first her own sanitation, noting her snack time, and being certain no one touched her stuffed animals who were joining the flight with us.

We managed to receive some grace and passed through with only slight interference, but I sensed the aura of tension building around Hope. We boarded the plane, and Hope and I settled nicely into our seats and pulled out our games, coloring, and favorite snacks. My heart rate increased when I noticed in my peripheral vision a bouncy photographer coming our way all happy and skippy, sporting his Goofy ears. I tried to glare at him to signal he shouldn't approach. Man, doesn't anyone pick up on social cues anymore? I soon discovered that Hope had a few choice words in her vocabulary awaiting such an occasion.

After one more awkward obstacle out of the way, we were soon airborne. Hope dozed into a nice little nap as the hum of the plane settled her into a sleepy rhythm. All was well in the world again. Then the speaker erupted to announce a special landing ten minutes ahead. I wondered what they meant by special. I was soon to discover that we landed in the middle of the airfield in Orange County at John Wayne Airport.

We were greeted by the mounted police, the Dream Lift crew with all their delegates, and, of course, a red carpet to exit the plane in royal fashion for all the Dream Lift candidates and caregivers. This was a day to celebrate the gift! To make dreams come true for all these children who face challenges daily and don't often get the chance to have full access to the world's most famous park for kids. OH NO! Hope had never been about the fuss. She preferred things quite simple and a little less noisy.

Instantly, she shot to her feet, and the questions rolled from her tongue quicker than she could articulate. "What is this? Who are all these people? Why is there a carpet coming out of the plane? Why are people wearing those things? Where is Disneyland? I don't see it! I don't like all of the noise! Why are there buses? I am hungry! When do I get to eat? Where is the food? Who do I have to sit with on that bus?"

I stared at Hope, rendered totally speechless. This was the time to pray. Hope begrudgingly followed the annoying crowd off the plane, but when we stepped off the red carpet and onto the tarmac, we faced another assault. A boisterous, bouncy, ball of fire ran toward us with pom-poms, a tweeter whistle, and a huge loot bag filled with goodies for Hope. I was terrified! Much like myself, this woman in costume wanted to be a hero. But when she drew near to Hope and I, the Dream Lift buddy halted in disillusionment when Hope closed her eyes and shut out the entire world.

I got pulled aside with an inquiry, demanding an explanation why Hope wasn't providing anyone with the response they were hoping for. I also noticed how little airtime Hope was now getting as they recorded this amazing day on live television for Wendy's restaurant lovers to see. Editing out Hope took up more time than the actual filming. Surprisingly, it became rather comical from my end of things, but I knew I needed to protect Hope and limit her from all this commotion. Hope opened her eyes to my quiet voice and asked to get on the bus so she could sleep because the whole day was exhausting her. I thought that was a great idea. It seemed like forever before the buses pulled out to make our way to Disneyland, but shortly after, we arrived at our destination of choice.

Excited, Hope had fixated on this part of the adventure for days on end and couldn't wait for the best ride at Disneyland. On our arrival, we would rush to the Indiana Jones ride, where we would dodge life-threatening boulders and duck through dark caves on our mission to get through the obstacles of the Indiana Jones quest for survival.

Hope and I exited the bus with a skip in our step, the Dream Lift enthusiast following at a safe distance behind en route to Adventureland. We rounded the corner where the map marked the ride location, only to arrive at a sign reading CLOSED FOR REPAIRS. I looked at Hope as I read every part of her soon to explode body language and interrogating rants about how this could possibly be a "dream lift" without the Indiana Jones ride?

She screamed at the highest pitch of her vocal range. "What is the point of life when this ride is out of order? Who did this? Where is the guy to come and fix it? I want my money back!"

Every Disney character got an earful of disapproving statements about the stupid, broken ride. I jumped in with a quick and easy diversion to the ice cream stand and the haunted mansion. Hope now focused on a potential recovery for our day—food. Meanwhile, we noticed all the glares and stares coming our way by other park attendees, responding to our obvious disapproval of a few things.

Hope and I got into a good rhythm again. We managed to circulate through the rest of Adventureland, Frontierland, and Fantasyland, enjoying roller coasters and teacup rides alike. Then we decided it was a good time to rest and have some lunch. The salad bar buffet was a mile long. Hope enjoyed choosing all the delights for her gourmet salad, topping it with a variety of seeds, nuts, feta cheese, and beets. This girl has a mature palate and an eye for good healthy food choices. We sat and enjoyed the atmosphere while we ate our lunch.

Following lunch, we only had a couple of hours before we would be heading back to the bus to catch our flight back home. Hope was aware that lunch was the big meal, and it was by far the best part of her day, and that time was coming to an end. We cleaned up our tray and dishes and proceeded back outside, still considering where to go next—Tomorrowland or the underwater submarine.

As we walked across the courtyard, Hope stopped and grew quiet. I attempted to connect with her and get a read on her motivations or anticipation, but I couldn't break through. So, I slipped my arm into her arm thinking we could lock in and maybe skip back to Main Street or into the lineup for the submarine ride when suddenly, her fist comes out of nowhere and clocks me in the face like a bulldozer to the nose! "OUCH!" I was taken aback, and then I watched Hope elevate to an unfamiliar level of anxiety.

She ran toward a metal chair, lifting it up into a perfect launching position aimed at me. I quickly responded and grabbed the chair, wrestling it to the ground, and then out of self-protection, I had to put Hope in a hold on the ground to calm her down. Here we are, blood splashed, inappropriate language vaulting into the magical atmosphere, and over to my left is Luke Skywalker and his little light-saber trainees staring in absolute stillness at the Dream Lift friends wrestling on the cobblestones.

I yelled for help a couple of times, but all I received were cutting, judgmental glares from the bystanders, wondering what I could possibly be doing to this poor young girl. It seemed like an hour had passed before a familiar face turned the corner and rushed over to us. She was one of the first-aid attendants from the Dream Lift Team. Hope instantly responded to her empathetic gesture and ran over to her arms, declaring that I was terrible to her and that she needed to get away from me.

It became apparent to me that no one on the safety crew read Hope's file and was up to date on her potential pitfalls. I gestured to the physio to go ahead and escort Hope back toward the bus while I dragged my bloody, scraped, and disheveled self behind, now referring to my day as more of a "Wendy's nightmare lift."

An hour before, I never could have imagined her behavior. Hope and I had photos taken of our hands in the air, screaming in fun on the roller coasters, and cute pics with all the characters, or at least the ones who weren't interrogated for making us wait in line for any period. Honestly, I felt for Disney Princess Ariel as she instantly became Hope's least favorite mermaid, and everyone knew it when she closed the line just before Hope's turn, to take her shift break. I thought Hope was going to toss her off her seashell and launch her over the bridge and into the fountain.

Hope did everything to avoid my company for the remainder of the trip. I had my justice moment at the airport watching the entire airport security team try and reason with her to check her bag and scan her hands. Everyone in the crowd could now witness the difficulties I had navigated throughout the course of the day. Not as many people glared in my direction. To top off our adventure, Hope delivered a passionate "F" bomb to the final report just before we boarded the flight home.

I imagine viewers will never get to see the true live footage of Wendy's Dream Lift in full action. I wish I had recorded my version; it would have been a new hit release for sure. All the children were exhausted and the caregivers even more. I sat a few rows over from Hope on the flight home and watched her settle from her extremely anxious state and fall asleep once again to the hum of the plane.

Sober, humbling thoughts washed over me as I reflected on our Dream Lift journey. Who was the trip really for? How did this experience set Hope up for success? What was I thinking? Was I a wanna-be hero? What kind of hero was I? Impulsive, adventurous, but a bit naïve and unaware of how Hope would respond to all the changes, the lack of sleep, the overstimulation, and the big disappointment of her favorite ride being closed. Had I considered all the things her body was going through with her hormone injections, new medications, puberty, pain from arthritis in her knees, and many other problems? The trip was never Hope's idea. She responded to the excitement of everyone else's excitement for her.

It was a huge, exhausting challenge to fly to Disneyland and back in one day, plus her experiences at the park. A dream kind of day for Hope was a cozy book to read on the couch, a healthy snack, a hot cup of tea with a friend, and a walk with my dog. I was no kind of hero to Hope that day, but she taught me a few things about how to be heroic. I learn more from her about what matters in life with every moment spent. I love that girl!

CHAPTER NINE

Unity

"The significance which is in unity is an eternal wonder."
—Rabindranath Tagore

Have you ever been surprised by God answering your prayer? He has answered many of mine, and it disarms me as He continues to hear me. This year I prayed that God would give me a word to hang onto, to pray into, and to focus my chaotic thought life to a place of beautiful simplicity. Well, He did!

While attending the Mosaic conference in Los Angeles, I was inspired by people gathering from different corners of the world who were willing to line up for blocks to come together and reconnect with the hope, the truth, and the power of God—God who knows our past, our present, and our future. The one phrase that resonated in my prayers was a heaven-on-earth mindset; I pondered it and prayed into it. Shortly after, God placed on my heart the word *unity*. He not only gave this word for me to think through, but he challenged me to live it, to choose to do life "with" those I share tension with or reject. He challenged me to choose to not be offended. I thought that sounded easy. *I can do this. Heck, I was a kindergarten teacher for years, and I have this "hug it out" practice down.*

Here I sit, honestly scanning through the motivations of my heart since I received this notion from God. I know my heart well, and I don't always like what I see. I have never been more aware of my brokenness, but the difference I now see is that it is only God that can make my heart a treasure. In every conflict I have had since this revelation from God, I have wanted to respond in not such God-honoring ways. But there's been an evident divine resistance within me that has silenced my fight, turning my eyes back to His picture of unity.

When God looks at my heart, he sees an instrument made for His glory, which has all I need to live unoffended by the power of His Spirit. He has this way of drawing me back to the story of the cross and what it represents for all of us. The power that the cross offers lies within us; it exists within our faith and our choice to believe in this miracle-working God. We make the choice—a simple yes or no. Our scattered emotions and all that informs the endless, negative scenarios that run through our minds have no power over the Spirit of the living God. He uproots our seeds of doubt, calms our fears, and walks beside us into the unknown.

I often pray that God would get me out of His way. I often feel that I am a stumbling block to this power when I try to decide the order of things. I pray that He softens and readies my heart to see beyond my scope of understanding, trusting fully that He will use all things for the good of those who love Him. We limit His power when we divide our communities to foster our own ideas of what is good and true and noble.

I often contemplate what one church would look like if we set all our differences aside and focus on the things that we have in common. Diversity of gifts, but the same Jesus. Every human on earth craves intimacy, purpose, and fulfillment. Is there such a world where we can make room for the diverse expressions of our individual lives but stay centered on the love of God and one another? I believe the gospel invites us to a divine journey that shows us another way, contradicting the nature of our humanity, the seduction of the world, and leading us into our God-given design.

God has used the places and faces that I've judged and rejected to show me the way to unity. He has orchestrated a divine shift within me. The very place I create the "us and them" mindset is where His power lies. I am aware of some now and I am sure He will reveal more as I remain open to learn. I feared girls when I was growing up who were engaging in risky behavior like substance abuse and promiscuity. I felt like I was making better choices than them and that I would never hang out with the likes of them.

It is humbling to admit this, but it has been a part of this prayer journey I requested from God. These girls bullied me in high school. They threatened and spread rumors, leaving me vulnerable and fearful most often. Never did I consider why they behaved this way toward me or what story might be behind their behaviors.

Now, one of my greatest gifts and passions is to be invited into a community of vulnerable women recovering from human trafficking, exploitation, abuse, addiction, and many other mental and physical health challenges. I work with an organization called NOW Canada that provides new opportunities for women who are struggling in these circumstances. I am a facilitator in the "Essentials" life skills program, focusing on building self-awareness, character formation, a shame resilience mindset, positive psychology, expressive arts, and more to help grow thriving, independent women who are working on a sustainable recovery and becoming strong contributors to society.

One of my favorite exercises is leading the women to consider their stories. I provide them avenues to channel their pain, to shift their thinking, to be able to share their story in a way that transforms. There are universal skills and talents in the world that are cross-cultural and trainable, but there is no story the same as any other out there. Their edge is in their stories. Their impact emerges from the stories they choose to tell themselves and share with others.

Now that I have heard many stories among these vulnerable women, I wonder who is learning more in this community? I realized why there are many stories of division I experienced as a young girl. I realized that authentic vulnerability is the best instrument to achieve unity and leadership. I am humbled by the student I have become as I pay attention to the journey of recovering women, overcoming shame and guilt from a life of transgression, seeing the hope in a redeeming God. The women of NOW Canada have challenged my assumptions, offered me grace, shown me how to ask for help, and taught me the power of vulnerability along the journey of healing and authentic self-discovery. I am so grateful to them all.

I have attended Alcoholics Anonymous and Narcotics Anonymous meetings in celebration of some of our graduates' celebratory milestones in their recovery, like the "one-year cake." Family, friends, and others sharing the recovery journey gather and speak truth and life into the individual being acknowledged. This is experiencing real church! Judgment was left at the door and brokenness embraced within a climate of encouragement and dignity. I felt loved by a community of women who had lived quite different lives than mine.

Some words of wisdom shared by my friends in recovery: Kat told me that ego meant "edging God out." I see ego weaved throughout my entire life, and God gradually reveals those areas to me and helps me surrender them more and more. Katee said that the difference between us and God is that God never tries to be us. Tina always encouraged me by pointing out that life is about progress and not perfection, something I need to review in my heart quite often. Jordie challenged expectations as she realized them to be premeditated resentments. Kayla asked, "What are you willing to do today that will get you where you want to be tomorrow." That question served as a gentle reminder to me that everything begins with intention. Brandy phrased it bluntly. "Wendy, own your own shit, man. And do the hard work!" Amen. Katee now comes to church although it's a long drive for her. Her response to my remark about the length of her drive was, "Do you know how far I used to drive for my drugs?"

I am so grateful for the NOW Community, including the incredible staff and volunteers. I believe in the women who participate, and I know that God will use them in significant, dignified, and powerful ways to bring hope and inspiration to the world if they choose to allow Him into their lives.

I am also ready to admit that I used to judge terms like "art therapy." I couldn't wrap my head around people who spent so much of their time painting or creating when there were so many responsibilities that nag. What about work? What about having a clean house; preparing healthy, balanced meals; exercising; grocery shopping; and all the "to dos" on our list?

I've changed. Now there is nothing I crave more than the space to create, the time to connect to the Creator, letting go of all restrictive mindsets and expectations, and diving into the wonder of capturing life in a snapshot of color and design. I love to help others to consider something new, to be inspired, and to explore unique self-expression.

So, I find myself asking, what is it that I really want? Do I want to single out the colors, the tribes, the pronouns, the talents, the gifts of other people, or do I just want to belong and allow others to belong? Do I want to concentrate on my pain, or do I want to count what is right in the world at the end of the day?

Do I want to remain stuck in the past and resent old memories? Do I want to fear the rampant spread of Covid-19, dementia, Alzheimer's Disease, or worry about socially distanced loved ones? Or am I willing to do anything to connect to the recollection of my journey called humanity and all that I have learned regardless of the feelings that infused the experiences?

Do I really want to keep score with another, or when that person has one more minute of life left, does my heart just want to notice all that is good and true about the gift of an individual who lived some of this life with me? And is it my hope that he or she will know the love of Jesus?

Do I really care how cool my church is and how trendy our worship songs are, or do I just want to be part of a community that authentically cares, prays, and believes in the best of me and the truth that the gospel offers all who invite Jesus to be Lord and Savior?

Do I really need the final word, or do I just need to hear the undertone of a divine love that makes everything worth it? I am realizing every moment of my life has worth if it is shifting and shaping me into the image of love.

Do I really want to spend my days, hours, and minutes, considering all the ways I can keep score, pay back, or set something apart, or would I rather be wide awake in the moment, fully present with the ones God has given me, seeing them as beautiful, broken, and vulnerable? I have learned I need to leave all the petty stuff to a big God who sees way beyond my scope of reason and leads me into something more substantial in my surrender.

Recently, our community was challenged by a leader who had or still has, depending on the perspective you choose, great influence among the most vulnerable in our city, teaching us how to love the least of these guided by biblical principles. Many looked up to him and created a pedestal for him on which to stand for all his noble work. They thought he couldn't possibly fall from such a place. Well, inevitably, he fell. His story caught up to him. Inside, there was a space that he hadn't worked through; it presented itself to him in a surprising way that caused a fall from leadership. It devastated him and many others. He said to me, "Wendy, you don't realize how much Jesus really is until He is all you really have!"

We often notice a special gift in someone and then place that person on an "expectancy" platform that will inevitably crash, launching many gifted individuals into dangerous places. It is easy to watch them fall sometimes, as often these positions can be threatening or envied by many—a sad situation but so true in this world. The church can be so quick to respond to this brokenness, sometimes in ways where the guilty deed is hushed, and that person encouraged to resign and gently fade or go away. Or the church may cover up the story in such a way as to save all who facilitated the fall. We can use platforms like this to feed gossip through poor, intentional prayer requests, priding ourselves on healing prayer rather than the dignity of all sinners, each of us included in that.

We proclaim that as Christ's church it is "ok to not be ok." Is it really? How are we protecting our leaders? They are human too. I still feel a heaviness in my heart for my friend—a friend who fell away for a time and is finding healing in a miracle-working God and through a small, authentic community that genuinely believes in the "roof crashing" heart of the Father. I anticipate how God will use this experience to teach our city a new way, a way that most won't have the courage to walk.

I wonder if this vulnerable church community can show us how this roof-crashing spirit can walk alongside a broken leader, loving that person and befriending them without shame, allowing them the grace to heal within the same community they once led.

A mentor and friend of mine is cofounder of this church's community center. She has many gifts to serve our vulnerable people in Kelowna. Her leadership inspires me as it is marked by love and modeled with grace. She is showing me what Jesus would do in difficult situations. She continues to speak truth openly and continues to love the sinner, leaving the reconciliation of the sin to a big God. She recommended I read *Barking to The Choir*. Gregory Boyle, the author, invites us to consider the power of "radical kinship." My friend offered me the same words she lives, where there is no "us" and "them," there is just "us," sinners alike, needing a savior.

My prayer is that we will watch and learn from what is painful and hard in leadership and how easy it is to taint a person's character who has risen to a high position. We all need to remember that we are on the same playing field in God's eyes. Let us receive the magnitude of His healing power in our lives as we do life with one another, sinner to sinner, heart to heart, glory to glory. I feel God will use this judged and vulnerable community, often rejected by society, to teach us something more substantial—something more about His devastating kind of love that overcomes.

CHAPTER TEN

A Storied Way

"Stories are the precious songs of your heart."
—Pastor Phil Collins

Story is an ancient, daily practice that gathers people to share cultural traditions, create legendary tales, and to ponder the future. Stories emerge from a mix of experiences, personality, education, culture, and character that was molded and crafted in the era and space that revealed our significance and influence over self and others.

Western civilization has Hollywoodized the process of telling stories with various platforms like movies, radio, media, expressive art, formalized education, public stages, and other forms of contemporary culture and technology.

Recognizing that the formation and presentation of the story may have changed, the root from which it began has not. Story time is rooted in the need to connect that is the process of noticing and the hope to inspire a response. The heart of the gathering—the storytelling circle—creates the connection.

Jesus models storytelling all through the New Testament. The beauty of His teaching style is firstly, it requires one to deeply notice something that creation has offered us to see in that moment. Jesus was the master at "deeply noticing," or particularizing what was unfolding directly on His path. Jesus, equipped with the heart of the Father and motivated to build the kingdom of heaven, was able to consider a way to draw in His listeners to hear the truth.

Jesus spoke in parables to illustrate a moral or a spiritual lesson, inviting the listener to a deeper posture of paying attention. Within the analogy of His stories were transferrable principles that connected to the human experience at large, but open enough for the individual to apply to his or her own personal experience. Jesus told the parables and left them with the people to ponder in their imagination and thoughts in hopes of shaping the hearers as they listen to the Father's heart. I believe He hoped to create curiosity about a new way of thinking and living, to draw His listeners to the idea of what it meant to live as a beloved child of God. Jesus was the ideal storyteller for us, but He also offers us the power to be ideal storytellers in our own circles of influence. He invites us to consider our own deep change or shifting experiences, which can be observed in our own learning and growth. When we take the time to pass on our stories, we offer the listener a gift—the gift of ourselves.

I was a kindergarten teacher for a few years, and "Show and Tell" was the highlight of every day. I set some rules around this sharing time. It was not an opportunity to bring something or brag about the latest toy or trendy technology, but rather it was a time to share moments, things, or people that meant something to the kids, inspired them, or shaped them in some way. It was the opportunity for all of us to get to know one another better.

We learned about the many talents the students had outside of the classroom. We learned about adventures they went on and what they discovered. We saw rewards they received from their hard work achieving a goal, and we heard about what they were passionate about. We learned how they spent their free time, their family traditions, about their fears, and so much more. But the most important thing of all in spending this time together was that we learned to see things differently to connect to one another more meaningfully.

Recently at our church, I was invited to ask people in the congregation if anyone would like to share a "shifting" moment in their life. This moment meant a time when an event or experience occurred that brought them closer to Jesus. To share a time when Jesus felt real and tangible to them. I had no difficulty finding the storytellers.

I found it more challenging to narrow the story down to sharing one "shifting" moment rather than an entire testimony.

That experience made me realize how much people want to share, to belong, to build meaningful communities around them. This little shift in church service traditions awakened people a little more. It liberated the quiet ones to find people they could identify with more easily within the church, and it removed some assumptions that many of us make when we don't understand why a person behaves or orients a certain way. It connected our community by heart in subtle and beautiful ways, such as sharing stories in different ways, sharing a poem, a piece of art, a song, or a photo.

All people have embedded stories in their hearts because we all have a way of relating to being human. I often find myself dreaming of what a "Story Church" would look like. Perhaps we could sit in circles and not rows. What would it be like if we invited all to contribute to the thoughts emerging from the process, and then have the courage to ask the tough questions? What kind of shift would that be in church culture? How many people would be baptized declaring Christ as their Lord and Savior?

We all have certain unique attributes that we share with other human beings. We share a level of compassion or empathy. We have intellectual abilities and the capacity to learn and grow. Every human being has a creative craving to express an awakening and a direction. We all have a way of imagining things that have not yet come to be. Faith...hope. What are your unique qualities that you contribute to the human story, to this grand narrative that God created us to write? We can't spend all our time in rows, attending webinars, and listening to podcasts, becoming overinformed and over motivated without expressing our own creative inspiration to make sense of our own lives.

What kind of story do you want to tell? Most people forget the facts they learned in school or the principles and theories of endless debate, but they rarely forget a good story and how it made them feel. God is patiently waiting for you to offer your gift and inform the world with what you imagine.

Paul reminds us in the book of Galatians that God sets us apart through our story. He works in those stories where He initiates our faith, those places of transformation. My pastor, Glen Madden, calls these "your against-all-odds stories." Our stories have been developing since God breathed life into our existence. Some of us can articulate our stories right away because we receive a message in our hearts from God, a revelation as Paul states in the book of Galatians. And others like Job, Abraham's wife Sarah, or Joseph ponder and pray about the *why* of their lives for years, sensing God's power but not receiving the promise as they hoped...yet.

In Job's case, he never received the answer to his suffering until eternity. We may never know all the intricate details of our story of transformation, but in faith we must trust that God does know. God reveals it all in His timing. It is our opportunity as we live in the world to pay attention to the power we sense in our souls, to the initiating presence of something more at work than what we see. We need to put on our spiritual ears, spend time in the gospel of truth, and enjoy a relationship with God. At the right time, He will reveal His harvest of righteousness in our stories.

An example happened in Damascus when Paul was stricken blind and received a revelation from God. That was his against-all-odds story. He went from persecuting people of faith to turning Christianity into a worldwide faith that was open to all. He did not waver from this heart change. Paul's evidence of his edge in his story is in the fact that he wrote three-quarters of the New Testament with truth of the transformational power of the gospel.

So, now we understand story to be one of the most precious tools for discipleship. Our stories are a source of building our depth and meaning in relationship with God and others.

One thing that burdens me greatly as a member of smaller communities for most of my life is the sad state of culture that chains people to the worse moments of their stories—the morally unacceptable places. The juicy gossip somehow makes us feel better to indulge someone else's pain to possibly shed ourselves in a better light. We often don't allow a rewrite of a person's life. We don't extend a person the grace to create a better ending to their story, to finish strong, to mark the world differently than with their most humbling moments of shame.

I hear more than my heart can handle through the stories from our women of NOW Canada that do the extremely hard work in their recovery, return to their hometowns only to be reminded of the pain they caused when they were engaging in an unhealthy addictive lifestyle and the devastating choices that emerged from those dark times. Too many experiences like this result in a relapse or an overdose of narcotics. I have officiated a funeral and attended many celebrations of life of young women who never got the chance of a re-do. They were never given the moment of dignity to shift their lives in a better direction, to know the truth of love and forgiveness, and to throw off their feelings of unworthiness.

This angers me, burdens me, challenges me, and sometimes keeps me awake at night. But it offers me the opportunity to examine my own heart and consider where I might be responsible for holding people captive in a story that divides us.

Included in the back of this book is a workbook that you can use, sharing some tools to build your "shift" stories and to share your experiences with others for impact. Hopefully, it will cause a ripple effect of the deep connections of the human experience at large, encouraging us all to a strong finish within our own story. This may offer you a few life-transforming, rewrite opportunities, or possibly begin the memoirs of your own spiritual renewal. Enjoy finding your unique "edge" in the process.

CHAPTER ELEVEN

Grief

*"For we are God's handiwork, created in Christ Jesus to do good works,
which God prepared in advance to be our way of life."*
—Ephesians 2:10

*"Should you shield the valleys from the windstorms,
you would never see the beauty of their canyons."*
—Elizabeth Kubler-Ross

I appreciate the quote above by Elizabeth Kubler-Ross because most of my life I have lived in the narrower valley of the southern interior of British Columbia within the Selkirk Mountain ranges of the West Kootenays, in a small town called Castlegar. This is where I spent most of my childhood and teen years.

I love to take my family back to the Kootenays often but especially in the summer. We gather all the family and whichever friends are available, and we float the Slocan River Valley, tubes under us, cold beverages in hand, and the current pulling us all in the same direction. My oldest brother Darren is always equipped with flippers to rescue the odd lost shoe or a person catching an eddy in the wrong direction or heading toward a boulder or tree. My brother Grant makes sure we all have a cold drink to sip on, takes count of the buddy system, and strategically positions himself to navigate what lies ahead. That might be spontaneous sightings of bald eagles, the mountain peaks, and the sound of the rushing water along the rugged riverbanks.

The peace is broken on occasion with "Someone grab Grandma!" Grandma in her blissful wonder knows someone will always pull her back to where she needs to be. She sips on her cider and enjoys the adventure. We usually pull off halfway down the river into a swimming hole, diving into the crisp, fresh mountain runoff, filling our souls with the freedom and joy of being one with nature. We often top off the day with some good food, drinks, a little music, and maybe some games and stories embellished with laughter. An all-around, good Kootenay day for all.

Now I reside in another small city, located in the southern interior as well, called Kelowna. It is embedded in the Okanagan Valley. I have lived in Kelowna for a little over twenty-one years now. If you ask people who live in Kelowna one of their least favorite things about it, many will reply that the seasons of cloud inversion are challenging. We can be socked in under a cloud cover that lasts for months. So, a conclusion that can symbolically be drawn from my geographic location thus far is that I have spent a lot of time in a gap or a valley, considering our big God and what He is up to in my life. Living in these areas I have experienced many shaping and molding opportunities as someone once referred to as the "Land Between."

I have become more personally connected to grief these last seven years through the loss of what I considered dream jobs, precious loved ones, and some failed health resolutions. Each one shifted my perception of life in different ways, especially the assumptions I carried about God. One thing I know for sure is that grief looks and feels unique and different to everyone, so I will not try to package something so precious into theories and boxes or statements that disparage.

However, I feel I can share some of my stories of grief in times of painful loss, challenges, betrayals, deep hurts, and loneliness. Maybe through my sharing, you may feel liberated to explore your own grief from a different perspective.

Many people wonder why our God of grace and mercy allows such terrible things to happen to good people. A fair question I would say. But my pastor and friend Glen provided me with some insight into this worldly blanket statement. He said, "OK then, if you take God out of the situation completely, what changes? Does the cancer instantly go away? Does a marriage heal? Does the sick child get better?" Not likely I thought.

He continued, "But if you put God back in the story, one now has hope." Hope is what we all need. These worldly conclusions about God often reveal the unwillingness of a cultural mindset to dig deeper and work to find out for themselves who God is, rather than follow some popular opinion, or take a stance on a line or two from Scripture pulled out of the context of God's complete story. Eternal decisions deserve a little bit more time and attention.

As I was growing up, I found I was susceptible to many thoughts about what grief should look like and how we should cope, informing my life in inauthentic ways contrary to my own natural process of grief. Often society has a quick-fix mindset to patch grief whether it be with a couple of counseling sessions, a pill, a diagnosis that stifles a person's self-understanding, or provides a health model that will cure all. Don't get me wrong. Some of these tools are very helpful, but there is a form of personal grit and faith required to transition through seasons of grief.

If I were to describe grief in the way I understand it now, I would refer to it as a state of being where lies a mystery that draws us to more revelation. No opinion, or alternative perceptions, or quick comfort attempts, or prescribed methodology can really settle the soul in personal grief experiences. The grief experience itself offers insight into our unique challenges, our biased perceptions, and the direction we choose to take our thoughts. The mystery and the challenge of grief offers us a choice. Do we box God in, or do we trust the greater scope and quality of God's plan?

Our culture can often model ways to stay "stuck" in our grief. Often, we move too fast to notice grief affecting people around us. Many are not able to articulate their personal grief and bury it deep inside, then cover it with endless distractions. Some lose sight that there is a better future of healing that is available through faith in a loving God.

I was exposed to many habits of the heart that occurred during times of grief that led many people I loved down challenging and less than ideal paths. I have seen people numb grief because they don't want to feel the pain, the loss, or change the way things used to be. Others lean into their grief stories and become codependent on the roller-coaster emotions of existence.

Grief always demands a reaction; our opportunity is to choose the right one for our best future—for our strong finish. This requires us to identify the tools and processes to transition well through the seasons of grief. This grief journey or wilderness walk looks different for each of us, but ultimately, I believe it is the landscape that offers us a deep, personal relationship with God. God draws us into a quiet, contemplative space when we grieve, gently inviting us to question what our source of joy is in this journey of life. Every time you experience grief, whether it be through pain, disappointment, betrayal, loss, or any difficult transition, you decide who you want to become and what you choose to believe.

The questions I repeatedly hear from God as I continue to transition through moments of grief are, "Wendy, will you trust me?" "Wendy, am I enough?" In these seasons, a strong source of strength for me is the Scriptures. Abraham is one ultimate example of trust in his Creator when God requests him to sacrifice his own son. I wonder whether I will ever grow to trust like that, but I fear to ever be tested like Abraham. Abraham's pivotal moment confirms God's faithfulness at an unfathomable level.

Consider the story of Joseph left in a pit, speaking about painful betrayals, and the years it took him to discover how God would use those scary and torturous times. He didn't go on a rampage of revenge or cultivate bitterness in his heart, holding his brothers captive to the betrayal story. Instead, Joseph chose to rewrite another ending to the story, one that brought reconciliation.

My pastor refers to Joseph's pit in the form of an acronym. He encourages us that P.I.T. stands for a "person in transition." I am beginning to see that any time I doubt, fear, isolate, or shrink in my life as I process grief, I can return to Scripture and read again about the heroes of faith who ran their race well. Here I witness God's faithfulness over and over and over again. The greater the challenge, it seems the greater the victory story. Maybe I need to look at the struggle as an opportunity for victory instead of paying attention to the feeling in those moments.

The other thing I discovered as grief seasons came and went was my journey to honestly explore my view of God. So many today find God in many forms to create a guaranteed feel-good life. Others picture God's big, pointed finger in the sky keeping score. Some can't even fathom a God who allows bad things to happen to good people. Many feel God is the great shame dispenser, tracking all the things they've done to earn His favor, gauging who gets into heaven or not. Some gods are identified as any form of pleasure. Some gods are formed powerfully in our manifestations of what is important to focus on moment to moment.

Where do these views of God originate? How has our Western world built such a sad story of God? How much of this have I internalized? I have grown to realize that my personal views of God will surely impact how I relate to Him and others during my times of grief. I am realizing as I transition through grief that some of my views of God need to be shifted a little to align with what the gospel tells me. I need to choose to look closer, dig deeper, and put on my spiritual ears to hear with discernment. It is not an easy task but a necessary one.

I would say that I first experienced what I would define as grief when my ten-year-old friend Marissa died in a nearby sandpit that all the neighborhood kids played in. Kids die! What kind of God does that? I also learned that bodies are delivered in odd-shaped cars, and my friend was getting put in the cold earth to lay there forever. I knew pain that I couldn't even find the words for at the age of ten.

A few years later, my high-school boyfriend got in a bad car accident and became paralyzed, compromising his dreams and goals for his future. I wonder if he knows this God of the bible. I wonder if he trusts God with his circumstances. I wonder what type of decisions he makes in his pain or time of grief?

My own health challenges became more pronounced in my teens, leaving my mind in chaos, asking endless questions. So many people seemed to know the answer to why I had this condition. I was either being punished by a God who was disappointed in my character, or I had to make amends in my faith journey. Maybe my mom took a drug that caused my condition, or I was a result of some mutation. The list goes on.

As I continue to walk with the "thorn in my flesh" (2 Corinthians 12: 6-7), God is stripping away all the lies and inviting me to trust Him. I know that God doesn't want me to be in pain or to be sick, but the fall of this world and the ripple effect of many things like genetically altered food and pollutants in the air, creates brokenness in every shape and form. Mine manifests in a syndrome (KTWS) that impacts my health.

This offers me a choice. I can choose to numb myself, which on occasion I am more than tempted. I could be a victim and focus on all the things that are wrong with me and burden all who will listen and carry out my agenda for me. I could choose not to live. The key is, I have a choice. We all encounter choices every day that will inform our future and how things will play out. I choose to believe and trust God with my health. Recall from earlier in the chapter, I chose to add hope into my situation. I am ok if I don't find out why my pain has not been cured in the way I hoped for. I have informed myself on options I have for some relief; ways I can continue to build my strength; and how to use my skills, God can take care of the rest.

I am choosing to write about this more freely since my encounter with David Roche at a local philanthropic lunch earlier this year. Before David took the podium, he noticed my daughter and I sitting at the same table. He locked eyes with mine and gave me an inviting smile as he walked over to introduce himself. He was quite curious about Hannah and expressed joy in seeing a young girl amidst such an older crowd at this luncheon. He asked Hannah how she became a part of the community and what her interests were in philanthropy.

Hannah offered a refreshing and honest reply, stating that she was taking this opportunity to learn about how community can impact change. She went on to share how she has enjoyed being a part of multiple community events that our family supports. She told David she doesn't know exactly where she fits in the big picture, but she is loving various experiences that are leading her into new opportunities to grow and be involved.

Then David turned to me and asked why I was there. I told him that I have been a recipient of great generosity in discovering my health diagnosis, and once one knows that kind of generosity, it changes you and it becomes a part of something you hope to pass on to others. I continued to share that I have the same syndrome as him, except mine is in my lumbar spine and right leg, within the main nerve routes.

David has clusters of vascular anomalies in his head and face, leaving him visibly scarred and in a position to always have to explain to people who ask about his awkward facial expressions. He put it this way, "I have my shadows on the outside, Wendy, and you have yours on the inside. You need to talk about yours!"

David rocked my world a little with that statement. I was growing bored of my story, and frankly, I didn't want to give it that much attention because it just felt painful and distracting. For most of my life, I felt that we gave power to the things we paid attention to, and I certainly did not want to give this problem more power than it already had in my life. Something shifted in me that day, changing my view of sharing my personal struggle. I feel now that it may bring hope to others, that life can be full, and infused with hope and compassion when you risk authentic vulnerability and share stories of struggle and courage. It often inspires others to give it a go as well. Thank you, David Roche! You are an angel on earth.

As I choose to trust God, He shows me the treasure that lies in grief. The most important is He has shown His deep love for me. When I come to the end of my own resources, He meets me there and reveals to me something so much more than I could imagine. He has given me a spirit of wisdom and revelation in the knowledge of who He is in my pain. He has given me stories that will bring hope to others experiencing pain in their own lives.

There is a band called I Am They who wrote a song called "Scars." In the song they allude to the wounds being the stories we will use to share God's heart. The scars will tell us who God is. How would we learn to trust God without a circumstance that required us to?

How would our faith walk be real without a personal choice to make? Consider an arranged marriage for yourself or the opportunity to choose your life partner. How would God's love be real to us unless we knew life without choosing it? God delivers us with every challenge we surrender back to Him. Jesus' scars tell us timelessly of who the Father is and His promise for us. So, I choose to be thankful for my scars, to share where appropriate, and I trust God with the rest.

On our trip to Africa, we were invited to consider a different perspective on grief. Africans feel human emotion very much the same way as we in the Western world, but they have a different posture around grief—a quiet strength, a reverence, and a peace. The way I explain that is they have much more opportunity to experience loss, grief, challenge, and pain in the Third World. They have many occasions when all they have is God, and they learn to lean into His hope alone.

The African Savannah offers a much different way of life than we experience. The brave warriors of the Maasai courageously fight through many circumstances where they must prove their bravery amid unfathomable difficulty to save or help their people. Death by multiple causes was and often still is a way of life. The cost of gaining access to opportunity is beyond our scope of understanding in North America. As my family spent some time sharing our stories and walking the way of the warrior, we discovered the conditions of their livelihood resonated with us and were mysterious beyond the land we were walking on. God is much bigger than the African landscape, and the people trust far beyond its scope.

It is also surreal and tender to watch loved ones walk through grief when we lose someone in common. I notice that my brother Grant tends to grow contemplative and quiet. His words are often expressed through a melodic acoustic guitar song, his emotions emphasized in tempo, gentle rhythms, and varied tones, leaving the listener to hear something within themselves and drawing all into a shared story. His music is so beautiful it is hard to express in words. He sits by the river, mesmerized by the birds and the majestic mountains, listening to life and forming concepts that he carries about the land's pain and wonder. He feels so deeply, he often cannot articulate his experience unless invited. He is so unimposing in his grief, yet so compassionate through it.

Some loved ones have offered more of themselves in serving others as they grieve, or sometimes set up related fundraisers to honor loved ones. Some have gotten busier and more distracted, and some have grown more isolated and philosophical. The human response to deep pain has an endless array of expression, but each one is precious and important, offering us all stories of hope.

God invites me to look at grief differently now. He is shifting my focus from my pain to something more. Paul says in his story that "to live is Christ and to die is gain." That is quite a shift in the grief perception, one that I pray God shapes in me. He uses our pain and struggle for a compelling journey of becoming people of authenticity and deepened faith. I now ask God daily to increase my faith, and I invite you to join me. Together, we will be amazed, even devastated by His love!

CHAPTER TWELVE

Take Flight

*"...they will soar on wings like eagles,
they will run and not grow weary,
they will walk and not faint."*
—Isaiah 40:31

I am at the age in my life now that I might be having a midlife crisis opportunity where lost dreams are worth chasing after, or the grass that looks greener needs some exploring, or I can lose my identity as the kids move out, leaving mom as the classic empty nester.

Our culture embeds in us mental pictures about life transitions that hardwire a story we are all supposed to live out and experience. I can say things like, "You're finally of legal age, or you're fifty, or you're retiring, and when your kids leave home, an empty nester!" All these phrases ignite a mental picture for you as you read them and anticipate these occasions in your own life.

I will play the dangerous assumption game and say that not all those pictures paint an ideal or an experience that leads you to a fulfilled life or the life you dreamed of. I guess one determining factor in your perception would be how you define ideal or success for yourself.

In my interactions with these milestones, I recall legal drinking to be the exciting milestone of nineteen, but it was a tad more fun to try to get into a bar when I wasn't old enough to be honest. The concept of the "grass is greener" is a world of illusion, as Dad would phrase it, that demands nothing of you, requires less commitment, and less grit and ownership, making it sound like a better way.

At fifty your life is half over. Did you accomplish everything you expected? What is your life amounting to? What is your purpose? It often seems like an age of mental chaos of reflections, expectations, and unfulfilled dreams. My husband, who works as a wealth manager, often hears that retirement for many sounds like a book on a beach, copious rounds of golf, and traveling to an exotic place with no demanding schedules and the luxury of living life at their own pace and rhythm. Among all the shared visions and interpretations of these milestones, there lies an identified truth. Retirement requires quite a mental shift and a behavioral change to transition well.

Lately, people are asking me the classic question. "You are, or are almost an empty nester now, so how are you handling that?" If I paid attention to how many others were handling it in my circle of influence, I would say that it would be in my best interest to stay distracted and busy; go back to work; or allow my emotions to run the course and have some good cries accompanied with bottles of wine. I do have the few odd friends who are celebrating their newfound freedom. Their house stays clean, the demands of life have slowed, the fridge stays full, the emotional day-to-day caregiving responsibilities have lifted, and their bank account is building.

I have a labyrinth of reflection that this new life transition has imposed on me now that it has arrived. I am forty-nine years young, and my eldest daughter Hannah has moved out, finishing her fourth year of business and finance. Our youngest daughter Madison has moved into a little casita on our property that is an independent suite from our home, and she is attending her first year of business with a marketing focus at the University of British Columbia, Okanagan. Both the girls have their own vehicles, their schedules are ever changing, and they are creating their futures. So, some things are obvious for me in this season of life. My role as a mom has changed. With that my learned behavior requires a bit of a shift. To be honest, I get stuck sometimes in the tension of what that looks like when it comes to curfew suggestions, daily rhythm setting, inviting them over for family dinners, checking in for a coffee, how much I listen versus how much of my thoughts and perspectives I offer.

Then there is the reflective part of this stage of life when I ask if a strong foundation was laid and if enough tools were provided to set them up for success. What exactly did the girls pay attention to as we attempted this thing called parenting? What are they noticing in our lives and what perceptions are they drawing from us? What questions did I not ask? What questions do they still have? Am I creating time to meaningfully connect with them? How is their faith journey going? Will they find their personal intimacy with God? When? How much influence do I still have as their new circles are forming and new experiences are happening without Mom and Dad? Is there a misunderstanding that has never been reconciled? Wow! My mind is filled with questions and reflections even more than I thought.

The wonder for me is that my husband and I were raising our girls while we as individuals and as a couple were continuing to work out our own stuff. We were figuring out who we wanted to be as individuals and how that would make freedom to thrive in a marriage. We were learning more about this personal relationship with Jesus, whereas before we went to church on Sunday, prayed privately, and memorized some good practices of faith.

We were often overwhelmed by the learning curve of family responsibilities, running our own businesses, the effort needed to keep a marriage healthy, managing finances responsibly, and navigating all the world's distractions. All of this, while parenting these two little girls. We only knew at the time what we knew, but some of those things have changed as we've grown more to discover who we are, who God is, and what God is up to in our lives.

But what will Hannah and Madison take from us to inform their choices going forward? This is the mystery of the empty nest for me. What will take flight in their lives from all we experienced as a family? What experiences have they not shared because some of them aren't funny yet, as my good friend Janice would say? There are outcomes I hope and pray for, but ultimately, I have no control over them.

One thing my life has certainly taught me is that mystery is only made known through experience. Our girls must experience life their way; sometimes that is what I fear. It is not the thought that because they aren't living in our home that I have no life without them. I have always invested in my passions and used my skills outside of the home while we raised our girls, leaving me quite a smooth transition into more time and freedom from the demands/rewards of parenting young girls.

The time for God's mysteries to be made known to Hannah and Madison in a personal way will be discovered in their own experiences. God is in control of everyone. The world offers us many choices and that leaves me vulnerable to the choices my children will make. Depending on what those choices are, there are always consequences—good or bad. My husband and I always prayed that the girls would live life from our shoulders, seeing beyond what we were able to offer. I imagine the heart of every parent is the hope that consequences don't cost a child too much. We also hope our shared wisdom helped prevent some difficult learning.

Vulnerability is probably the best description of how I feel in this new transition. I, along with my daughters, am vulnerable to the trends, distractions, and influences that shape a woman's life today. So many distractions linger and overwhelm, requiring us to take time to reflect and savor solitude to navigate them well. Our everyday demands and self-imposed expectations rob us of the needed, quiet practice of reflection, and the time to unleash our creativity. The ever-shifting patterns of relationships and circumstances are unstoppable, influencing and shaping our thoughts and opinions of who we are and who we hope to become. The heart of a mom is to have some control over these shaping opportunities and to direct the mindset of our children in what we define or perceive as healthy, morally gauged, and good for their souls.

Over time and conversations with God I am realizing more and more how I get in the way with my ideal plan of shaping or influencing others. My plan is not always His and is limited by my perceptions. I tend to act based on a small God, narrowing my own faith journey. I am reminded in Scripture that He is the master potter. He loves Hannah and Madison more than I do, and His plan always proves to be better than mine. These last few years God has allowed me to struggle and feel pain at new levels, but He also has led me to victories that overcome the pain. He has expanded my scope of who

I understand Him to be. How many times has He done this for me? I am just starting to grab hold of the magnitude of His promises.

My prayers have increased in number. My husband and I pray every morning for our girls, and our focus has shifted for them. We have placed into God's hands the burden of responsibility that we could never bear in their story. I choose to trust Him with Hannah and Madison, even though it feels like a tug-of-war sometimes. I know my daughters are uniquely gifted. They are kind, courageous, compassionate, and generous young women who have confidence in their skills. I have no doubt that their lives will be rich with meaningful relationships, opportunity, and growth. Trusting God is becoming enough for me today, and there is such freedom in giving over my life to Him! May you find freedom in trusting Him with all those tender places and people in your life too.

This is not a season of crisis with my identity, but more a time to confirm my identity. I have a better understanding of what it means to be a beloved child of God. My nest isn't empty; it is more of a drive-through for whomever is passing by wanting a little love and hospitality. My girls are two of my favorite people in the world. They are a priority of my heart, so we spend precious time together. It may come in spontaneous moments or various dates that work in lives that are moving in many directions but with the same focus, en route to creating a meaningful future. I let myself imagine the impact these two beauties will make in this world, and I pray that I get to be around to participate in their journey.

Life plays out according to what we pay attention to. These past few years have shown me, often in very painful ways, that when I pay attention to the struggle, the "fix it" strategy, or the cultural mindset, I am emptied and grow weary and can feel anxious. But when I set my eyes on Jesus, the one who endured the worst conditions of the human experience for me and settled the score for all on that cross, I am freed from fear, my assumptions, and control.

Finally, I am understanding who God created me to be and what it means to "be still and know that He is God." I was given that Scripture by a nun when I attended a silence and solitude retreat in Nelson,

BC more than twenty-five years ago. She told me that it was God's heart for me. I believe that the Scriptures are timeless. The words of Paul and all the characters God used in the formation of the Book of Life are living and active, crossing over time, distance, culture, and trends, reminding us of our loving Father, the source of the beginning and the end. If God is for us, who or what can possibly be against us? What is left to fear but God himself? We only need the courage to shift our focus to the true source of all that is good, powerful, and finite. If we take the courage to run our race well, we will all meet in the champion's circle in the end. And what a celebration that will be!

"No, in all things we are more than conquerors through Him who loves us. For I am convinced that neither death nor life, neither angels nor demons, neither the present nor the future, nor any powers, neither height nor depth, nor anything else in all creation, will be able to separate us from the love of God that is in Christ Jesus our Lord."
—Romans 8: 37-39

Now that's one good ending to our story!!!

CHAPTER THIRTEEN

Pause

"Be still and know that I am God."
—Psalm 46:10

My husband Grant and I recently returned from a month-long vacation in San Pancho, Mexico. We craved solitude, a quiet place to get back in touch with ourselves, a time away from screens, people, and the vast array of stimulation that our world offers. We were leaving little margin between the events of the day, placing our bodies into a state of anticipated urgency. We had some big decisions to think through, needing less influence and popular opinion regarding our personal health and the next ten years of our career paths. We had never done such a thing before. We often take holidays with family and try to maximize on the adventure of exploring new faces and places, but once back home, we need time to recover from our vacation.

After this last time away, we both were humbled by the realization of how good this retreat was for us and how less can be so much more. We were embedded in a jungle on the Pacific Ocean, one hour north of Puerto Vallarta, where we were surrounded by deep, rich palms and tropical birds. We were a fifteen-minute walk to the beach or to the little village, leaving us to enjoy the natural rhythms of the day in our time with God, in our solitude, and with one another. We took the opportunity to fill our spirits through our morning time with God, being influenced by His word and studying the fruits of the Spirit. We did a deep dive into each attribute of Christ's character, and we were invited to offer a different response with our own lives, creating great contemplative opportunity and conversation over our morning coffee.

I prayed for God to give me a word, one powerful word, that I could conceptualize and apply in my journey of faith and relationship with Him. The last time He gave me the word "unity," as I mentioned previously in my book. This time, I was frustrated with the word I felt He gave me. I continued reviewing my heart to see if this word was really for me. As I read through Scripture, prayed, wrote in my journal, painted, and took long walks and talks with my husband, the word wouldn't go away. Are you ready for it? Restrain! The word was "restrain!" What? Me, the crazy blonde, a whirlwind of energy, soul barfs, and maker of "to-do" lists? Yes, I feel this is my word because I'm sure God meets us in the sacred place of our imaginations if we allow Him. There, He can show himself to us. He met me there with an invitation to respond differently with my life going forward. "Wendy, restrain and trust me."

I felt an invitation to embrace a resting kind of faith and recognize my distorted sense of urgency in certain areas of my life. God wanted to intervene in my "fix-it" mindset and remind me once again of a familiar Scripture—"be still and know." I am also awakening to the possibility that experiencing restraint or limitation can lead to creative renewal and a growing faith.

God invited me to "shift" how I see the challenges in my daily life from relationship struggles, to lack of funding options for essential services for our vulnerable community, to lead team expectations, to raising young adults in a world that is in moral chaos and leadership confusion, and to my own ongoing health challenges. I needed to restrain myself from defaulting to my own tools and my way and shift my heart to Christ's way. I needed to reimagine my life with a lighter posture, a curious anticipation, and a possibility mindset.

In San Pancho, Grant (Deli) and I woke every morning to the sun streaming through the windows and to the sounds of the exotic jungle resonating in our souls, inviting us into an eternity of promise in God's word. There are unique and endless gifts within us that God wants to strengthen and align as we find intimacy with Him. If we want our lives to be dedicated to Kingdom purposes, we must consider first who we are in God and how we respond in love to our circumstances.

Others need to feel, witness, and experience the fruits of the Spirit that point them to a compassionate, miracle-working, and pursuing God. In our world today, suffering is experienced in diverse and personal ways—ways that tempt us to doubt God, shrink into ourselves, or get caught up in the monetary happiness of new stuff, endless pursuits, or the use of numbing agents.

Instead, we need to restore suffering, hurting people to the truth that each person matters so much to God that He sent His only Son to die on a cross for each individual person, no matter the age, race, or human condition. The cross radically transforms how we think about suffering as the measure of what God truly values—reconciling all of us to Him and building in us a new creation. This human condition of suffering requires healthy community and the reminder that we are one body and one spirit. We cannot live out our life choices based solely on feelings and circumstances. We must shift our mindset to believing in the existence of a BIG God who is involved in all the details of our lives and uses all things for good for those who love Him.

We returned from Mexico about a month or so ago, and we are right in the middle of the Covid-19 pandemic, a strange and mysterious landscape in many ways. These types of health crises seem to occur every one-hundred years, the last one being the Spanish Flu pandemic.

We are already recording the things that mark this pandemic experience for many. Here in Kelowna, an evolving season of innovation and creativity is bursting forth, with distillery factories shifting from making whiskey to turning out hand sanitizers. We have seen drive-by birthday celebrations, and multiple platforms of virtual faith, family, and community gatherings like Zoom. We hear repeated requests to stay home, stay safe, and practice social distancing; an endless array of face mask designs and colors; the notorious toilet paper because how can we survive without toilet paper? Store shelves are constantly emptied of sanitary wipes and bleach.

We see more families spending time together than ever before and understand that there are more families with domestic challenges than ever before as well. Many are baking, especially banana bread or sour dough. Residential properties and yards have never looked more manicured. There are invitations to bring your own chair and sit six feet away.

Now we stand on large dots on the floor and say no more. The media in our homes is bombarded with political sensationalism. All celebratory events (graduations, funerals, weddings) are canceled or postponed. Now there are many Facetime goodbyes to loved ones who have the virus and are quarantined or in the hospital.

Now virtual concerts and porch entertainment are shared within neighborhoods. People gather across the nations to make noise at 7:00 p.m. to share gratitude and respect for health care workers and first responders—heroes on the frontlines—who are risking their lives as we navigate the scary waters of the virus. A virus that does not discriminate by age, race, city, or country. Meat hoarders are being bashed on social media. There are endless Covid-19 posts from the latest and the greatest source. There is breaking news of more lockdowns, closures, businesses going under, statewide quarantines, and more.

Horrifying TV images flash across the screen of body bags that have been left in buildings, refrigerators, and stockpiles, waiting for space and a dignified closure to a precious life. There was a massive shooting in Nova Scotia uniting all of Canada in an even more intimate form of grief over innocent lives lost. There are many new renditions of old songs like, "The Lion Tweets Tonight," trying to relate, comfort, or bring a laugh to the human heart.

Colored hearts are displayed in the windows in support of community helpers decorating the neighborhoods and reminding us that we are all in this together. People are calling loved ones, trying to offer any service they can and trying to support local small businesses and neighbors. The walkways have random painted rocks or signs with words of hope and inspiration. Some liquor stores are placing restrictions on purchases in hopes of not creating an addiction risk that could serve to numb the pain of this crisis time for some people.

Family game night is rebirthed, and dinner is back as the main event. Spending has slowed, the stock markets breed fear, the future of many people's retirement savings is unknown. My girlfriends joke that we will finally learn one's true hair color and natural face wrinkles without fillers. There are endless Tik Tok challenges; my husband and I even attempted one.

The word God gave me in Mexico now makes a little more sense—restrain. Its power is much more meaningful in my life as I practice social distancing. I am trying to use just what we need during this time, finding creative ways to encourage others and to bring hope. I am trying not to allow my imagination to take over with all the scary anticipation ahead, and much more. This is an opportunity to be transformed by the renewing of our minds, opening our hearts to God, and inviting His shaping power in our lives. I am inviting him to produce more fruit of character and compassion in my life. Optimistically, it is an opportune time to practice unity and love.

I learned as I studied the fruits of the Spirit that they are just that, the fruits of the Spirit, not of Wendy. Without God's power in my life, I remain in my own brokenness. Each time I live outside of a compassionate response, the more I limit His loving power in my life. So, I have learned to pray differently too. I pray daily for God's Spirit to change me on the inside from a person who tries to do good and fix things, to one who is divinely able to do good things. I surrender my thought life to Him and ask for the strength to always shift my eyes to Christ. I want to embrace a deep longing for Holy Spirit joy that sustains me in all circumstances and overcomes all feelings of anticipation, pain, or fear.

I want God to use every situation in my life to reveal to me something more about His amazing love. I am reminded about the pieces of my heart that I have held back or "restrained" and have invited God into those spaces of control, practicing my trust that He is in the details. I have learned to seek out my patience and to practice it with intention by establishing a daily rhythm of habits that cultivate this for me. I wake up early, and I find my cozy place by the fire with my frothy, Breville espresso and Bible. I read the Scriptures with my husband, we discuss them, and then we pray together. I journal what I feel God is highlighting for me personally in that moment. I then take my dog for a walk and ponder God's thoughts, intentionally noticing His presence in the calm lake, the clouds in the sky, the sounds of the neighborhood, and the fresh air. Each time, it feels like a gratitude walk for me.

Then my day is a series of ninety-minute bursts of work and responsibilities until the dinner hour arrives. This is a non-negotiable space for my family to gather, to break bread, and to share stories of the day, connecting, imagining, disagreeing, or whatever it offers. Then the pace and activity slow for the evening. This time for me usually involves another walk as the sun goes down, a dip in the hot tub, and/or a creative or quiet activity. It is a new way for me that cultivates *Shalom*. This rhythm is challenged more as the world crisis amplifies, but I am reminded of the wise words by Joyce Meyer that "Patience is not just an ability to wait. It's really about how we behave in the waiting."

I took my study a little further and asked myself some courageous questions. I did what Pastor Craig Groeschel would call "an energy audit" and considered the things that got me off track—the stuff that makes me struggle with kindness and love for others; how I experience God's goodness in my life; how I measure growth; how I address my inner coward, and where I hesitate to share my faith; and when restraint is difficult in my life.

The list goes on, but this time allowed me to do a deep dive into my mindset, my core values, and how they aligned with my actions. I asked God to reveal to me where this resting faith needed to be exercised in my life and what behavioral changes needed to be made on my part.

God's unchangeable character offers me an opportunity to respond in faith to Him with the people he has given me, the talents He has designed in me, and to the daily events where he leads me.

One of the fruits of the Spirit is gentleness. As I examined this term, I discovered the word "meek" was a major trait of gentleness. Through gentleness, God gives us restrained power so that we can always exercise compassion and a softness toward people around us. There is that word "restrain" again.

I realize that one of my strengths is "maximizer" from the Clifton Strengths Finder assessment and that indicates I am wired to always raise the bar, taking what is best and making it even better. This is in contradiction to meekness. Often, my strength as a maximizer can get me in trouble as I push for improvement. I can make others feel that they don't measure up. I need to use this strength in a different way, as ideally the true definition of a strength is when it empowers others to reach their own potential.

I realize more and more that I need to invite God into the details of my life daily, so that my strengths may be infused with His power to exercise consideration toward those around me. I ask God to continue to make me teachable, humble, and compassionate, so He can awaken the best in me.

As I complete this final chapter during my social isolation time during the growing pandemic, I sense God working in my life more powerfully than ever as I reflect on my journals, spend time in the Word, and try to live at peace in the tension. He is a faithful, enduring, and loving God. So, I feel His overriding peace, a sense of something bigger at work in it all, with every sensationalized newscast; with every uninformed expectation or assumption presented through world leaders; every awkward social distancing moment in the stores or in my neighborhood; and every theory that builds fear of the unknown.

I believe God gave me that time away and the word "restrain" to prepare me for this season of life. He knew the pandemic was coming. He made himself known to anyone willing to find Him in the crisis, and He offers us something far more substantial than anything this world can offer. I see glimpses of Him at work in a kind neighbor; in a church rallying to love the people in quarantine through prayer, delivering messages of hope, and sharing biblical truths during this time of uncertainty.

Our magnificent God is still at work, no matter the feelings the pandemic ignites. The sun continues to shine, and the sunsets have never been more spectacular. The snow and the rain fall in their own timing. The wind blows, and the power of nature follows God's design even as the world seems to be in utter chaos.

God possibly has allowed some of these things to invite a pause in our lives. Perhaps He is inviting us all to respond differently, to consider our ways, and to *shift* behaviors. This is a time to consider where our own lives may need pruning, to ponder the implications of indulgence, and our instant gratification mindset. Restraint.

H.B. London once said, "What we do upon some great occasion will probably depend upon what we already are! And what we are will be the result of previous years of self-discipline!"

Our faith is evidenced by our consistency to live out our core values with conviction; the daily surrender of ourselves; and following Jesus. I trust God daily to supply the power to live a faithful life. I realize more and more that this is a life practice, an accumulation of good habits. They include ongoing prayer, learning the gospel, attending a faith community, having accountability partners who will examine my mind and my heart, time away from everything for reflection, and an opportunity to practice all that I have learned.

It is the perfect time to pray courageous and bold prayers, knowing the Lord will offer us something more substantial than we imagine in our prayers. We are all in need of knowing a good God!

Craig Groeschel offers the perfect prayer. I love it because it isn't super long and hard to grasp, it resonates powerfully, and really says it all:

"Lord thank you for giving me someone to protect, a battle to win, and a kingdom to advance. God, I believe you will, I know you can, and if you don't do it today, I still believe."

Now let us pray that prayer with a trust we've never known before!

We are all in this season. I am grateful for the opportunity to grow amidst such a challenging and scary time, knowing that God is using it all for something good in us and in the world. I am anticipating something more substantial when we reach the other side of this pandemic SHIFT!

I have shared many of my shifts in beliefs, assumptions, and perceptions within this book. Now I invite you to pause, consider your ways, and what you choose to pay attention to as it can substantially change the course of your life's fulfillment.

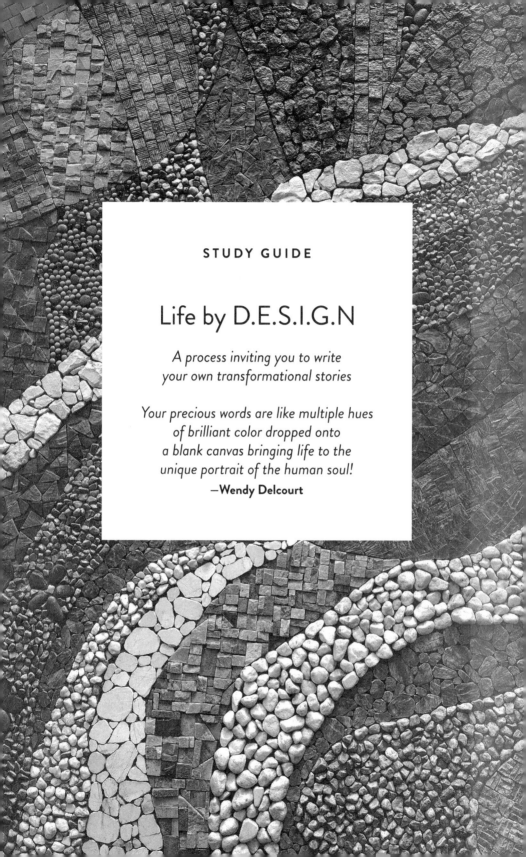

STUDY GUIDE

Life by D.E.S.I.G.N

*A process inviting you to write
your own transformational stories*

*Your precious words are like multiple hues
of brilliant color dropped onto
a blank canvas bringing life to the
unique portrait of the human soul!*
—Wendy Delcourt

Introduction

*S*hift...*moving toward God's perspective* is a compilation of how I have mused, reflected, and pondered events in my life over the last ten years, making sense of them as I process and respond to the shaping opportunities within those defining moments. I call it a process that invites me to consider the qualities of my unique design of personality, strengths, and gifts.

Even though the stories are biased by my perspective and understanding, they lead me to an inner peace regardless of the emotion tied to the experience or the reaction I had to each one. Ultimately, through this process, I discovered within me all the layers of my human journey living out the devastating love of God. He invites me to trust that there is richness and fullness beyond my greatest imagination at work behind it all. It really comes down to what I choose to pay attention to.

Being a teacher by vocation, it excites me to share this process with others to help them identify with their own pilgrimage of discovery. I believe the greatest legacy you can offer is *your story*. This process will reveal the *why* of your behavior, motivation, and direction, revealing the mystery of you to the ones who love you the deepest and care to pay attention to the beauty of your journey. I hope you find a common connection within the tender parts you choose to share.

Storytelling Tips—A Brainstorm—Story Web

(Gather your colorful pens and highlighters and prepare to unleash your thoughts or do a "heart belch" as I like to term it, onto paper with no rules or rhythm.)

I invite you to consider moments of success and motivation; consider unforgettable experiences; share where you have discovered some of your talents; consider some things you imagine that happened or haven't happened yet; consider something that helped you grow as you jot down one or two key words with each idea. This is mainly to brainstorm key events and as you go through the process, the questions will invite more detail and specific responses from you. Later, in the study guide, I will invite you to give more detailed and specific responses, helping you to shape an impactful three-to-five-minute story of transformation. My hope is that you will be motivated to tell your own stories using this easy writing process.

1. On a poster board or a tablecloth-size scroll of paper, believe that the ideal storyteller of your story is YOU! Write "My Story" somewhere on your paper.
2. Brainstorm and write every moment you remember in your life so far. See the invitation to consider some ideas above. Use two to three words to reference the moment. In your style, use as many colors or symbols as possible to connect to the thought.
3. Look for repeated themes, behaviors, and perspectives in your life journey. Have fun and maybe give them a unique name, i.e., I have a "Wanna Be Hero" or a "Grief" section in your story.
4. Identify the times and places when you experienced fear, pain, or mysterious emotions around a perceived success and/or failure. Circle the fears, box the pain, and star the mysterious places.

5. Find evidence of courage, creativity, and compassion. Mark those with a big purple "C" beside each.

6. Consider that your stories often identify with a deep shift or change experience. For instance, perhaps becoming more empathetic toward others through a challenge you've personally overcome. Can you title the shift experiences on your page? Have fun with this!

7. Stories are the desired curriculum needed to continue growth and development in the teller and listener. Highlight some of the biggest growth opportunities with a green highlighter.

8. Much of your story probably emerges from your pain and how you dealt with it, your hidden dreams, your fears, and maybe victories over some of those fears. Can you come up with some story titles around these?

9. You are giving your audience a gift. We pass on knowledge and differing perspectives for others to connect to. Do you recognize within your brainstorming those gifts of vulnerability, learning, wisdom, hope, or another that might be unique to you? Mark these so you can recall them, i.e., I may use an "L" to indicate a learning experience, or an "H" marking moments that created hope in my life. Choose something that works for you.

10. The story must be told in your natural style. There should be an evident connection tying your story together and a personal understanding of its significance. When you look at your brainstorming, do you understand more about why you experienced some of these things? Start a list of "whys" on the back of your page.

11. There needs to be a link or connection of a relationship with the story you're telling and your listeners or readers. The main points or themes within your story should be transferable to the personal experience of your audience. Can you identify common human experience within your unique moments—betrayal, shame,

insecurity, power, success, courage? List these somewhere on your paper.

12. A story should be three-to-four minutes in length and
    told at least fifteen times to master your communication
    style. Each deep change experience can be packaged into
    a three-to-four-minute story to share. Identify three or
    four of these events from your brainstorming map that
    you will develop into a story that you can share with oth-
    ers. List them on the back of your sheet of paper so you
    can reference them later.

13. Your story should give something away about yourself. I
    like to think of it as an appropriate level of vulnerability
    for your audience.

Things to consider when you share your story:

a. **Tone**—Varying pitches allude to authentic feelings and dynamic living.

b. **Eyes**—Connect visually with all listeners during your sharing.

c. **Space**—Lean into your audience from time to time as you circulate around the room. Stop and maybe sit at the profound moment.

d. **Characterization**—Animated sections help connect to human emotion. They bring life to your descriptions.

e. **Humor**—Amusing anecdotes can have a strong influence on your listener and add a compelling nature to a story.

f. **Pause**—Leave time when telling your story to consider the emphasized parts of your deep change experiences or areas that you want to highlight.

g. **Tempo**—Practice using a reasonable pace in your telling to keep people interested and engaged. Focused listening time is approximately three-to-four minutes.

Some potential story openers:

Have a read through the many questions below and **identify five** that resonate with your motivation to build on the concept. Write your responses in bullet-point form on the pages provided after the list of story-opener questions. Consider your brainstorming poster to help build your short-story content.

1. Who is a person in your life that you felt really noticed you?
2. Share an adventure that inspired you in a new way.
3. Share a courageous conversation you had to have and how it worked out?
4. Share a time when you were challenged to step out of your comfort zone?

5. Where have you felt the most vulnerable in your life and why?
6. Share a time when you wanted something badly and to what extent you went to achieve it.
7. Share an assumption you had and how it impacted your relationships.
8. Share one of your fears and how you are managing it, or not.
9. Share a passionate desire.
10. What sort of activity makes you lose track of time and surroundings?
11. What inspires you and makes you want more?
12. How would you fill your day if money and time were no object?
13. Share one or two ways you have dealt with conflict and its results.
14. What sorts of things burden you creating a desire to respond?
15. If you had a stack of books by your bed, what would they be about?
16. What has happened to you that changed your pursuit?
17. Who sets the compelling standards for your life and why?
18. What elicits a heightened response from you and why?
19. What prevents you from living your authentic self?
20. Choose one of your favorite attributes and imagine what your life would be like without it. Share your thoughts.
21. Who is a key person who informs your soul formation?
22. What sorts of things bring out the best or worst in you?
23. What story are you giving power to that is draining you?
24. What battle have you lost and how did it make you feel?
25. How have you discovered your purpose?

Choose 5 of the questions from above that resonated with you, offering you a story to share about yourself. Use the pages following to display in bullet-point form your thoughts when answering each question.

Story Opener #1

Stories are the precious songs of your heart.
—Phil Collins

_____

_____

_____

_____

_____

_____

_____

_____

_____

_____

_____

_____

_____

_____

_____

_____

_____

_____

_____

_____

_____

_____

_____

_____

Story Opener #2

We are not here to fit in, be well balanced, or provide examples for others. We are here to be eccentric, different, perhaps strange, perhaps merely to add our small piece, our clunky, chunky selves, to the great mosaic of being.

—Brene Brown

Story Opener #3

Only when diverse perspectives are included, respected, and valued can we start to get a full picture of the world.

—Brene Brown

_____

_____

_____

_____

_____

_____

_____

_____

_____

_____

_____

_____

_____

_____

_____

_____

_____

_____

_____

_____

_____

_____

_____

Story Opener #4

In order to write about life first you must live it.
—Ernest Hemingway

Story Opener #5

Do not judge my story by the chapter you walked in on.
—Unknown

_____

_____

_____

_____

_____

_____

_____

_____

_____

_____

_____

_____

_____

_____

_____

_____

_____

_____

_____

_____

_____

_____

_____

_____

MEANINGFUL CONNECTION

For stories to illustrate our big God at work and to connect with the universal human experience, they must be motivated by the following:

Love—Intended to encourage, build up, correct gently, keep unity with evidence of compassion and vulnerability.

Share Thoughts:

_____

_____

_____

_____

_____

_____

Liberating—Connecting in ways where the listeners feel safe to share precious stories too. It builds courage in others when the storyteller is authentically vulnerable.

Share Thoughts:

_____

_____

_____

_____

_____

_____

_____

_____

Leading—Influence in the direction of hope, trust, and faith.

Share Thoughts:

_____

_____

_____

_____

_____

_____

_____

_____

_____

_____

_____

_____

_____

_____

_____

_____

_____

_____

_____

_____

_____

_____

_____

_____

Leveraging—It stimulates a culture of deeply noticing others, nurturing meaningful connections that grow like a ripple effect. (i.e., if you ever experienced a chronic illness, you may now have compassion for another person who is going through the same thing.)

Share Thoughts:

_____

_____

_____

_____

_____

_____

_____

_____

_____

_____

_____

_____

_____

_____

_____

_____

_____

_____

"If your dreams do not scare you, they are not big enough."
—Ellen Johnson Sirleaf

LIFE BY D.E.S.I.G.N.

Our story is our unique **D.E.S.I.G.N.** I love acronyms as they help me remember key points in my teaching and practicing of these skills.

Jot down all the ideas that come to your mind as you consider the questions around this design acronym. Your precious stories are nestled within the responses. Use previous notes, story prompts, and brainstorming to inform your responses.

<u>D</u>.E.S.I.G.N = our **DRIVERS**
(Write down some of your thoughts in bullet-point form)

- **What motivates you?**

_____

_____

_____

_____

_____

_____

_____

_____

_____

_____

_____

_____

_____

- **What matters to you?**

  _____

  _____

  _____

  _____

  _____

  _____

  _____

  _____

  _____

  _____

- **What has happened that has changed your goal?**

  _____

  _____

  _____

  _____

  _____

  _____

  _____

  _____

  _____

  _____

- Who sets high standards for your life and why?

- What do you hope people will remember about you?

- What are your 5 top core values? (See values inventory page.)

_____

_____

_____

_____

_____

_____

_____

_____

_____

_____

_____

_____

_____

_____

_____

_____

_____

_____

_____

_____

_____

_____

_____

VALUES INVENTORY

To burn with desire and keep quiet about it
is the greatest punishment we can bring on ourselves.
—Federico Garcia Lorca

Values serve as motivators; they determine the direction we go and the intention behind our decision. By identifying our values (core beliefs), it helps us articulate what we stand for. If we don't understand our core values, we are vulnerable to destructive influence in a chaotic realm of possibilities.

Key questions to help you identify your core values

1. What bothers or agitates me? Why?
2. Who do I admire and why?
3. What do I take a natural interest in?
4. Where do I give my time, treasure, or talent freely?
5. What makes me feel safe?
6. How do I define success?

Ponder these questions and mentally map your responses. You might want to write them in your journal or notebook, considering them thoughtfully as you reflect on your life experiences.

Consider the words offered below, but feel free to choose your own words, and circle the top 5 values that you resonate with the most. Take into consideration that there may be some crossover or similarities in themes (i.e., learning and development) so choose the words best fit for you.

Achieving	Integrity	Creativity	Learning
Meaningful work	Relationships	Justice	Environment
Adventure	Laughter	Hospitality	Idealism
Affirmation	Communication	Status	Wealth
Healthy body	Efficiency	Consistency	Challenge
Faith	Generosity	Positivity	Open-mindedness
Community	Autonomy	Peace	Motivation
Passion	Stability	Freedom	Spirituality
Contribution	Respect	Connection	Development
Fame	Service	Mercy	Humility
Dependability	Knowledge	Wisdom	Curiosity
Courage	Influence	Intimacy	Kindness
Loyalty	Accountability	Diversity	Belonging
Intuition	Patriotism	Reputation	Leadership
Balance	Transparency	Authenticity	Confidence
Perseverance	Resilience	Harmony	Simplicity
Purpose	Family	Order	Love

As you reflect on the words that you have chosen, create a life purpose or strength statement that feels consistent, personal, and a reflection of a successful or meaningful life journey for you. This exercise is helpful when shaping your own personal stories for impact.

Example

A meaningful life for me is when I take courage to live with integrity no matter the circumstance within my relationships and commitments. I hope to remain curious about opportunities to grow as a person and to channel my passion and creativity toward impact.

> *Experience is the hardest type of teacher;*
> *it gives the test first and the lesson last.*
> **—Oscar Wilde**

D.**E**.S.I.G.N = our **EXPERIENCES**

Experiences are made up of your "lean-in" moments as they catch your attention in unique ways.

The story you tell, often birthed out of awe, mystery, pain, or difficulty (shifting moments) becomes the filter used when seeking growth opportunities.

Science teaches us, if we reflect on our experiences and challenge our assumptions, our stories will take on a new expression of who we are.

You are in charge of what you accept as yours! SO, WHAT YOU HAVE THE COURAGE TO BECOME THROUGH THESE EXPERIENCES IS THE KEY.

- **Describe an experience that awed you, or took your breath away and why?**

_____

_____

_____

_____

_____

_____

_____

_____

_____

_____

_____

_____

- Describe one of your biggest struggles and how you
  wrestled with it, recognized the "why," and made the
  necessary shift to reconcile it.

_____

_____

_____

_____

_____

_____

_____

_____

_____

- Share a fear experience and your response to it.

_____

_____

_____

_____

_____

_____

_____

_____

_____

- What experience demanded a courageous response from you and what did that look like?

_____

_____

_____

_____

_____

_____

_____

_____

_____

_____

- Where in your life do you feel you have to perform to be accepted?

_____

_____

_____

_____

_____

_____

_____

_____

_____

_____

• **Describe an experience that helped you realize your purpose.**

_____

_____

_____

_____

_____

_____

_____

_____

_____

_____

_____

_____

_____

_____

_____

_____

_____

_____

_____

_____

_____

_____

_____

_____

"What lies behind us, and what lies before us,
are tiny matters compared to what lies within us."
—Ralph Waldo Emerson

D.E.**S**.I.G.N = our **STRENGTHS/SPIRITUAL GIFTS**

(I encourage you to complete the strengths finder assessment at www.gallup.com to discover what you naturally do best. Visit www.spiritualgiftstest.com to discover your God-given gifts. Visit www.enneagraminstitute.com and complete the "RHETI" test to learn your personality type through an ancient personality type system with an uncanny accuracy in describing how you are wired.)

STRENGTHS

Marcus Buckingham defines strengths as "activities that make you feel STRONG." God placed them in you so you can master these activities, be empowered, and fuel others with that power.

- **Name your top 5 strengths and their attributes that best describe your WOW!**

_____

_____

_____

_____

_____

_____

_____

_____

_____

_____

_____

_____

- What strength do you see the most in your day-to-day activities, and what do you like best about it?

_____

_____

_____

_____

_____

_____

_____

_____

_____

_____

- Did any of your identified strengths catch you by surprise? Why?

_____

_____

_____

_____

_____

_____

_____

_____

_____

_____

- Out of all your strengths, what would you like others to notice at work in you?

- How will this new understanding help you add value to the endeavors you are already involved in?

- Do you see an area where your strength/s could get you into trouble?

_____

_____

_____

_____

_____

_____

_____

_____

_____

_____

_____

_____

_____

_____

_____

_____

_____

_____

_____

_____

_____

_____

_____

_____

SPIRITUAL GIFTS

In summary, these are themes of mercy, power, and word gifts—the parts of us that are amped up by the Holy Spirit for Kingdom work, so we can live and be the change we hope to see in the world.

- **Which of the following categories do you feel you best fit in serving others?**
    a. WORD GIFTS—encouragement, teaching, leadership, pastoring, apostleship, evangelism
    b. MERCY GIFTS—giving, serving, helps, compassion acts
    c. POWER GIFTS—wisdom, faith, word of knowledge, healing, miracles, discernment
- **Where do you see these gifts come alive in you?**

_____

_____

_____

_____

_____

_____

_____

_____

_____

_____

_____

_____

_____

_____

- Where have you been invited to practice your gifts?
  How did it go?

_____

_____

_____

_____

_____

_____

_____

_____

_____

_____

_____

- Do you struggle with any of them? Why?

_____

_____

_____

_____

_____

_____

_____

_____

_____

- Do others recognize anointed gifts in you, and how is that expressed?

- Is there a gift you wish to develop more? How will you do that?

"Thought that drops onto the canvas of your imagination
is now one that is breathing and living..."
—Ed Weiss

D.E.S.**I**.G.N = our **IMAGINATION**—the sacred place where God meets us to reveal more of who He is.

- **What are you giving life to in your mind?**

_____

_____

_____

_____

_____

_____

_____

_____

- **What activities make you dream and make your soul come alive?**

_____

_____

_____

_____

_____

_____

_____

_____

_____

- **How may you be limiting God?**

_____

_____

_____

_____

_____

_____

_____

_____

_____

- **Describe how your creativity comes alive?**

_____

_____

_____

_____

_____

_____

_____

_____

_____

_____

• Do you play? What does that look like?

_____

_____

_____

_____

_____

_____

_____

_____

_____

_____

• How are you staying curious?

_____

_____

_____

_____

_____

_____

_____

_____

_____

_____

"How wonderful it is that nobody need wait a single moment
before starting to improve the world."
—Anne Frank

D.E.S.I.**G**.N = **GROWTH**—how your shaping opportunities
develop your potential.

- **Who are you surrounding yourself with? How are they influencing you to be your best?**

_____

_____

_____

_____

_____

_____

_____

_____

- **Where are you actively seeking to learn?**

_____

_____

_____

_____

_____

_____

_____

_____

- Do you have mentors in your life to check in with the quality of your mind and heart?

_____

_____

_____

_____

_____

_____

_____

_____

_____

_____

- Are you practicing daily reflection? What are you noticing?

_____

_____

_____

_____

_____

_____

_____

_____

_____

_____

- Who are you following? Why?

_____

_____

_____

_____

_____

_____

_____

_____

_____

- Are you connecting to the source of truth and wisdom in your daily life? (Bible reading, prayer, authentic community)

_____

_____

_____

_____

_____

_____

_____

_____

_____

_____

"Strength does not come from physical capacity.
It comes from an indomitable will..."
—Mahatma Gandhi

D.E.S.I.G. <u>N</u> = **NEED**—What do you **need**? How are you identifying with your value and contribution to the world?

- **What makes you feel creative?**

_____

_____

_____

_____

_____

_____

_____

_____

_____

- **What things do you do fearlessly, bouncing back quickly if attempts don't work out as you planned?**

_____

_____

_____

_____

_____

_____

_____

_____

_____

- **Where do you naturally volunteer your time, treasure, talent?**

_____

_____

_____

_____

_____

_____

_____

_____

_____

_____

- **Where do you spend time so focused that the day flies by?**

_____

_____

_____

_____

_____

_____

_____

_____

_____

_____

- If you had a whole day, with no limits, to fill with whatever you want, what would be in that day?

_____

_____

_____

_____

_____

_____

_____

_____

_____

- Why has this book come to you now? What has brought you to this place on your journey?

_____

_____

_____

_____

_____

_____

_____

_____

_____

*"Your precious words are like multiple hues of brilliant color
dropped onto a blank canvas, bringing life to
the unique portrait of the human soul!"*
—Wendy Delcourt

Encouragement

(Review all your work and try to summarize the short stories nestled in the answers and reflections.) Begin with the ones that you feel you can easily talk about without notes or a time limit.

1. Package 4 to 6 four-minute stories that reveal a piece of you to the listener.

2. Practice the stories 10 to 15 times, hopefully not with the same person, to reach a mastery level of sharing it with confidence.

3. Keep a journal or a space to write down new stories as you come across them during the week. They are always there if you are looking for them.

4. Be a stellar question asker to foster the heart connection of storytelling. Use some of the openers I have provided to encourage a storytelling culture in your circles.

5. Look at yourself in the mirror and say, "My story is worth it; therefore, I will share it!"

*I hope this journey brought you closer
to God's perspective within your stories!*